A Journey to the Nature, Foundations
and Implications of the Gospel

QUESTIONING THE WORD
AN ATHEIST CONFRONTS FAITH IN GOD

JACK FORBES

JAFO PUBLISHING
375 Redondo Ave.
PMB 320
Long Beach, California 90814

QUESTIONING THE WORD
AN ATHEIST CONFRONTS FAITH IN GOD

Copyright © 2012

ISBN 978-0-9836418-0-3

Published in the United States by
JAFO PUBLISHING.

All rights are reserved, but for permitted use by the U.S. Copyright Act of 1976. Copyrighted © no part of this publication may be distributed, reproduced, stored or transmitted in a retrieval system, or transmitted in any form without the prior written permission of the copyright owner.

Printed in the United States of America © 2012

Design & Typography: Redmond & Associates
M. Redmond — K. Thomas — R. Korns
marioncreative@gmail.com
eBooks: rkorns@worthgold.com

Contact website information:
www.JafoPublishing.com

Preface

In examining one's own beliefs honestly, self-discovery should ultimately be the goal. Since religious beliefs are fundamentally based upon "faith," the most effective tool of persuasion may well be *questions*, or "food for thought."

I was raised a Lutheran, Missouri Synod, in Long Beach, California. As a boy, I was full of questions about everyday life—What's the secret to water skiing? Why I enjoyed team sports? Why my father wore suits to work? And why my mother's cooking was so delicious?

And as I grew up, my inquisitive nature turned to subjects of science and religion—Why we see only one side of the moon? How ants cooperate with such tiny brains? Why whales have lungs instead of gills? Why there's a God? Did the Red Sea really part?

Through posing questions to myself and searching for answers, I became interested in science, in people, in the workings of organizations, in social causes and in dealing realistically with the fact that my faith in Christianity was fading. By the age of sixteen, I played water polo in high school, surfed, played guitar, ended my baseball career (for the next ten years), started writing stories, took an interest in girls, and became an atheist.

Through the ensuing decades of my life, in speaking

with people of various religious beliefs and political persuasions, I couldn't help but notice that few are affected by being *told* answers. People, as it turns out, basically *don't like being pushed around*, intellectually or otherwise. Most people, however, *are* open to asking, then answering, **questions**—if they can *just get started* in that direction. Nevertheless, in many folks, there does seem to be a sort of **critical mass of intellectual inactivity** in need of a swift kick in the butt.

How many church-goers live in virtual denial of obvious issues inherent in whether to have "faith" in their particular religious beliefs? If one didn't know better, one just might think a ***stigma*** exists against self-examination of faith in the principles of organized religion. And if it's true that few Christians or persons of other religious beliefs are prone to critically evaluate their faith, then on an *international scale*, this could amount to a big problem. After all, for example, "Christianity" is touted as the central moral structure of many Christians' lives. Why doesn't it work, or at least why doesn't it work better?

In **What Is Your Question**?, *Scientific American*, March 2013, p. 12, Dennis M. Bartels refers to a Report by cognitive scientists John D. Bransford and Daniel L. Schwartz of Vanderbilt University pertaining to the nature of the learning process. The Report, according to Bartels,

"found that what distinguished young adults

> from children was not the ability to retain facts
> or apply prior knowledge to a new situation
> but a quality they called 'preparation for future
> learning.'"

According to Bartels, the Report further concluded that college students, unlike Fifth Graders,

> "had cultivated the ability to ask [insightful, important and probing] questions, the cornerstone of critical thinking. **They had learned to learn.**" (bold added for emphasis)

The questions in my book are intended, by their content and sequence, to stimulate formation and development of the reader's critical thinking skills and to thereby encourage meaningful and responsive self-discovery. In short, this book is intended to help the reader "learn to learn" regarding important issues of their religion.

So, with this **small book of big questions**, limber up your minds, jump into the probing realm of critical thinking and take a fresh look at whether your chosen religion *merits* belief—on the basis of pure faith or otherwise.

Jack Forbes
Author

Acknowledgements

This book may not have been written except from my long-standing friendship with Christopher "Chris" Hutchinson. Chris holds Christian beliefs, but has a significantly open mind to a process of self-examination. The book started out simply as an essay of questions to see if Chris actually **understood** what it was that he believed in. His willingness to engage in the ensuing discussions and the further issues which emerged from such discussions, motivated me to complete the book in order to afford others a similar opportunity of introspection enjoyed by Chris.

I would also like to thank Scritto da Anonima, author of *Divorce Stress Syndrome*, without whose guidance and advice on self-publishing this book may have simply remained in my computer hard drives. Chance meetings in line at a Post Office can truly have amazing consequences.

Dedication

Questioning the Word is dedicated to my loving sister Ginger who lived a joyous albeit tragically shortened life and to my mother Tottie, who was both a creative force and was independently and incredibly resilient in the face of adversity. Each of you has been a source of endless inspiration to me in my life adventure.

Table of Contents

Preface iii

Acknowledgements vi

Dedication vii

Table of Contents viii

Chapters   **Page**

1. Roadmaps—the Church Creed 1
2. Origins of Existence 10
3. God's Powers and Purpose 16
4. Miracles and Free Will 22
5. Souls 30
6. Evolution of Life 37
7. Spirits and Superstitions 41
8. Spreading the Word 45
9. The Literal Truth 48

10. God's Word to Man 52

11. A Woman's Place 61

12. Adam and Eve 63

13. Fundamental Rights 70

14. Heaven and Hell 74

15. Jesus Christ 85

16. The Creation Story 91

17. Noah's Ark 97

18. Life and Death 107

19. Faith and Verifiable Fact 110

20. Science and Religion 113

21. Implications................................. 124

JACK FORBES

1. Roadmaps—the Church Creed

Should your church have a *creed*—a set of core, key beliefs—required for membership?

Could an open, notorious and avowed atheist be a member of your church? Could 100,000 atheists join your church? Could those atheists change the core set of beliefs required for membership in your church? With this in mind, should your church have a core set of beliefs required for membership? What is the creed of your church?

Does your church have such a creed required for membership?

Is the Constantinople Nicene Creed[1] the creed of your church?

Specifically, what are all of the elements of the core set of beliefs which make up the creed of your church? Wouldn't you want to know?

Who establishes the elements of the creed of your church? Does your Pastor establish all of the core beliefs for your church? Does your Pastor establish *any* of the core beliefs for your church?

Do the current members have any say as to the church creed? How does that work, as to input by current church members?

Has some *hierarchy* within your church established your church's core beliefs? What is the hierarchy of your church which is responsible for establishing the core beliefs of your church? How is the hierarchy of church leaders appointed or elected? How do members of the hierarchy meet? When and how often do they meet? Is this a local, national or international hierarchy for establishing the creed for your church?

Have the core beliefs of your church ever *changed* over the history of your church? Is there any *record* of the core beliefs of your church over the history of your church? Why did the core beliefs change over time for your church? Is there a newsletter of sorts, announcing the latest developments of what you must believe in order to remain a member of your church?

May each member of your Congregation establish aspects of his or her *own* core beliefs and still remain a member of your church in good standing?

QUESTIONING THE WORD

If one of the core beliefs of your church is that the Bible contains the Word of God, does that mean that *everything* in the Bible is the literal truth? Is *anything* in the Bible the literal truth according to your church?

Are there stories in the Bible which depict events that never actually occurred according to your church's creed? Does the Bible contain any disclaimers that a particular story here, or a miracle there, are not factually accurate historical accounts? With God, is there truth in advertising, or is everything *caveat emptor*?

Does your church believe that all of the spoken words attributed directly to God, to Jesus or to the Holy Ghost are *actual quotes* from the respective deity?

According to your church's core beliefs, which parts, specifically, of the Bible are *not* the genuine and truthful Word of God? Does your church regularly circulate to its members a list of each of the factually baseless accounts within the Bible? Why not?

Is it up to *each individual member* of your church to decide which parts of the Bible are merely fictitious stories? If your church gives you the flexibility to have beliefs of your own so long as consistent with the church's core beliefs, do you *have* any such beliefs, of your own, concerning God? What are they? Do you ever share your *own, personal, beliefs* about God and the Bible with other members of your church?

Why does your church need a Pastor (or Pastoress, as the case may be)? As an aside, why is it that there is such a low percentage of female pastors of Christian churches?

What is stopping members of the Congregation from signing up to give sermons to the Congregation? Would this be a good idea? Are you as qualified as anyone to preach to the choir?

Why is Baptism important if faith in your church's creed otherwise meets the criteria for going to Heaven?

Are Catholics wrong when they claim that sins are divided between venial sins and mortal sins?

Do you believe that there are sins, known as *mortal* sins, which, if left without repentance and absolution prior to the moment of death, condemn the person to Hell?

Why would suicide be a mortal sin if a person is compelled by depression and despair to take his or her own life?

Why would suicide be a mortal sin if a person is a secret agent ordered by his country to commit suicide rather than be taken prisoner and interrogated? Are Christians ineligible as covert intelligence agents?

Why would suicide be a mortal sin if a person is terminally ill, draining the family of money from paying medical bills, wracked with severe pain and discomfort and wanting to die to end it all? Is suicide a mortal sin if expressly permitted by the laws of the country in which the suicide occurs?

Why would suicide be a mortal sin if a person was about to be torn apart and eaten alive by den of crocodiles breaking into a place where the person was hopelessly trapped?

Why would suicide be a mortal sin if it were necessary to save the life of another? Is it a mortal sin for a Captain to go down with the ship in order for one more passenger or crew member to be saved?

Do you believe Catholics are wrong to believe that there is a *Purgatory*—a sort of way station where deceased persons are assigned by God to Heaven or to Hell?

Do you believe that a person can become *stuck* in Purgatory for any reason—a sort of *stagnating prison* resulting from a speedy trial denial? Does the Stealers Wheel's popular song, "Stuck in the Middle" come to mind, as it does for me?

Why would there need to be a Purgatory if God is all-knowing? Does God have a difficult time making up his mind?

Is there any manner of *work furlough* program for deceased people stuck in Purgatory? Could a Witch Doctor free anyone from Purgatory?

Roadmaps—The Church Creed

Do you believe Catholics are wrong who believe that there exists a *Limbo*—a place where infants who die before they are Baptized—are sent? Specifically, what is Limbo?

Why would God consign any dead infants to a place other than to Heaven?

Is God mentally ill?

Is God cruel? Sadistic?

When (how early in their lives) are children responsible for faith in your church's creed in order to be saved?

If a Devil-worshipping cult member forces bizarre cult beliefs onto his or her children, could that constitute child abuse?

If a Muslim requires his or her child to memorize the entire Quran word-for-word, could that constitute child abuse?

If a Christian indoctrinates his children into the Christian faith through Sunday School, regular prayers and parental instruction that Christianity is the only truly genuine religious doctrine, could that constitute child abuse?

How old must a child be to be entitled to say "no" to Christian indoctrination?

Is there *any conceivable legitimate reason* for the people of The Sudan to have been embroiled in civil war for decades? Is Sharia Law anything more than a pathetic excuse to subjugate people to repressive and archaic Muslim notions of morality?

Are the ones who created the "God" notion simply ignorant people from a period of human history 2,000 years ago? 2,000 years ago, were societal institutions too unsophisticated, corrupt, weak or oppressive to give protection and identity to minority cultures and beliefs?

Have you ever considered the possibility that everything you have learned about your religion could be the result of an elaborate ruse developed and handed down over the ages by some combination of vested interests and well-meaning dupes? Can you keep an open mind as to that possibility being the reality? Does it matter to you whether the meaning of your life is based on a set of false beliefs? Is it blasphemy to *ask questions*?

Does your opinion count? Do you want your opinion in matters of life to count? Do you *want* the *freedom* to think and to express an informed opinion?

Why, in your opinion, is the First Amendment right of freedom of speech considered a *fundamental* right in America? Is the right of freedom of speech advanced, protected and encouraged by the government of Iran? Is the right of freedom of speech advanced, protected and encouraged by the hierarchy of your church?

Has your church hierarchy recommended this book, *Questioning The Word*, to your Congregation? Has your church hierarchy recommended *The Jesus Mysteries* to your Congregation? If the times, they are a-changin', how long before people stop oppressing and killing in the name of their religious fantasies? Is every religion except yours a fantasy?

In present times, have religions become anachronistic in leading and controlling behavior and morality in nations, states and municipalities? Have sophisticated and modern Constitutions, laws and judicial systems, combined with an increasingly informed and empowered constituency, relegated religion to an obsolete and perfunctory status?

---

[1] A common translation of this creed, developed by the Council of Nicaea is as follows: "We believe in one God the Father Almighty, Maker of Heaven and Earth, and of all things visible and invisible. And in one Lord Jesus Christ, the only-begotten Son of God, begotten of the Father before all worlds, God of God, Light of Light, Very God of Very God, begotten, not made, being of one substance with the Father by whom all things were made; who for us men, and for our salvation, came down from Heaven, and was incarnate by the Holy Spirit of the Virgin Mary, and was made man, and was crucified also for us under Pontius Pilate. He suffered and was buried, and the third day he rose again according to the Scriptures, and ascended into Heaven, and sitteth on the right hand of the Father. And he shall come again with glory to judge both the quick and the dead, whose kingdom shall have no end. And we believe in the Holy Spirit, the Lord and Giver of Life, who proceedeth from

the Father and the Son, who with the Father and the Son together is worshipped and glorified, who spoke by the prophets. And we believe one holy catholic and apostolic Church. We acknowledge one baptism for the remission of sins. And we look for the resurrection of the dead, and the life of the world to come. Amen."

2. Origins of Existence

Was all life on Earth created within the last 5,000 or so years by God? Since then did all life on Earth remain unchanged to present times?

Did all life on Earth evolve over time in a process initiated and directed by God?

Did all life on Earth evolve over time as a result of natural selection, not involving any input from any "God"?

Does your church believe in **Creationism** as to the origin of the world and of mankind?

Do you believe that Earth was created only some 5,000 years ago? Did God design all of geologic history to trick scientists into finding overwhelming evidence that the Earth was billions of years old? Did God place dinosaur fossils deep into rock to make it *appear* that dinosaurs actually lived, though they never really lived? Did God create the continents so they *appear* to have been connected hundreds of millions of years ago but where they really never were connected? Is the shifting of continental shelves an *elaborate illusion?* Are *Earthquakes* simply God reminding us that he holds our fate? Did God *sprinkle diamonds* deep into the Earth's core or were they instead created over millions of years by carbon compressing under enormous heat and pressure? Did God create *human* DNA so that it merely appears to allow for evolution by mutation and natural selection but doesn't *actually* work that way in Humans? Did God create distinct races of Humans with no *rational explanation* instead of races evolving by virtue of the migration of Humans to various parts of the world, and once there, experiencing natural selection in varied ecological conditions?

Did God perversely decide to challenge Humans' faith by creating an *endless supply of evidence* supporting evolution, when in fact nothing has ever changed from the moment of creation to the present?

If God gave Humans *an intellect and capacity to reason,* would God want you to **actually use** your God-given abilities to understand the world around you? Do you believe that God wants to *confuse* you and for you to *distrust* your sense of reality? Why would God want to turn Humans into slackers who ignore science and reason in interpreting the origin of life? Do you think that the Dark Ages was a particularly useful period in human history? Would you like to have the Dark Ages repeated?

Does your church believe in ***Intelligent Design*** as to the origin of the world and of mankind? Do you believe that God's hand was responsible for setting the physical realities of the universe in motion? Do you believe that God established all of the laws of nature?

Have you heard that nothing can be a "law" of science unless it never changes? Do you believe that a law of science would still be a law if it could be overcome by a divine intervention? Do you think that miracles are a *trump card* for God to change the laws of science in his unbridled discretion?

Has the sun risen in the West of the Earth at any time in recorded history? Has the moon failed to rotate around the Earth in your memory of events? Have the oceans of the Earth dried up any time recently? Have you ever heard of a tall building lifting off its foundation and floating in the air for 24 hours? Have the L.A. Dodgers had a winning season recently? Have the weak actually inherited the Earth? Despite the urgency of finding a cure for AIDS, has God spoken to anyone to reveal the absolute cure? Is there any proof that God actually created existence? Can you verify scientifically that God created the formula for Kinetic Energy? Does E always equal mc^2 or does God get to change Einstein's historic formula of the connection between energy, the speed of light and mass from time to time? Exactly what is the point of the Intelligent Design concept if laws of nature never change? What is the significance of the theory of Intelligent Design if it does not vary in any significant way from evolution following the Big Bang?

Does your church believe in **Evolution** following the big bang as to the origins of the world and of mankind? Have you ever subscribed to *Scientific American* magazine? Do you want to learn more about life and existence, or in your life do you try to emulate the ostrich sticking his head in the sand? Are you satisfied with "faith" establishing the basis for the rules of your life?

Do you feel that it's right for some Muslim sects to forbid women from becoming educated? What could possibly be the justification for arbitrarily depriving women of an education? Do you believe that it is acceptable for some Muslim sects to prohibit "Western" culture such as dancing or Pop music in their countries? Do you feel that it is appropriate to force women to hide behind veils?

Do you believe that a religious education is an appropriate substitute for a secular education? Do you strive to know the truth or do you believe that *"Ignorance is bliss"*?

Do you believe that history is filled with religious disputes and bloodshed? Do you agree that all religions cannot simultaneously be correct? Is your religion somehow the "correct" religion? Why are you so lucky? Why do you suppose each and every Protestant religious group (Baptist, Methodist, Lutheran and so on) believes that it is the highest and best Christian religion? Why do Catholics believe that

Catholicism is the true and purest of all Christian religions? Why are some Muslims fanatically committed to imposing the Muslim faith on everyone in the world?

Why do all religions require "faith" whereas science requires "verifiable proof"? Do scientific laws of physics (for example, the mathematical formula for Kinetic Energy) rely on *faith*, or on verifiable proofs?

Is there any verifiable proof of Immaculate Conception? Is there any verifiable proof that the Earth was created only around 5,000 years ago? Is there any verifiable proof that life as it existed before recorded history remains exactly the same today? Is there verifiable proof that God has *any influence whatsoever* in what occurs in the Universe? Is there any verifiable proof that God can and does create miracles? Is there any verifiable proof that prayer actually may lead to divine intervention?

Have you ever seen an apple falling *upwards* from a tree? Or heard of a broken porcelain doll spontaneously *reassembling itself* into an unbroken porcelain doll? Has anyone witnessed a crushed dog suddenly spring back to life? Is there verifiable proof, on the other hand, that the laws of nature are immutable (meaning, unchanging and ever-present)?

Do you believe that somehow people are different from all other forms of life in terms of their evolution or lack of evolution? When you hear hoofs, do you think Zebras?

Have you ever actually studied human evolution? Are you confused and skeptical each time scientists unearth a new prehistoric form of Humans, carbon-dated from further and further back in time and which appears to be closer and closer in appearance to the Great Apes?

Do you insist that once God set the Universe in motion, he gave up the reins, so to speak, never again to exercise any further influence over the Universe? If God gave up control over the Universe, is there any effective difference between Intelligent Design on the one hand, and Evolution following the Big Bang as the origin of life and the Universe on the other hand?

3. God's Powers and Purpose

Do you believe God exists?

Do you prefer simple answers to complicated matters of life and death?

Do you believe everything you read? Do you think a fair amount of skepticism may be helpful in life? Do you like to be told the answers, or to ascertain and verify the foundations of your beliefs independently? Do you prefer to understand why the answers are the answers, or to be given the answers with little or no comprehension on your part? Did you cheat in school?

Have you ever seen God? What does he look like?

Have you ever heard God?

Have you ever touched God? Did you report your contacts with God to the Associated Press?

Would you describe each direct contact with God you've had? Was anyone else aware of your direct contacts with God? Did you act on your direct contacts with God?

Are you a manifestation of God? Is Charles Manson a manifestation of God? Is your neighbor a manifestation of God? If everyone is a manifestation of God, what distinguishes you as a manifestation of God?

Does God speak with our country's leaders? If God tells our President to spend 500 billion dollars on a bail-out, should we simply go along with that, or should there be debate in Congress? Are God's instructions debatable? What if God tells *you* "X is always correct for everyone" and tells *your neighbor* "X is never correct for anyone", was God lying to someone? Why would God lie?

How many Gods have there been in all? Why?

Why did God create life? Why are Humans in the image of God? What is the image of God?

Can you describe what God is? Is God an all-knowing, all-powerful Creator?

If God is an "all-knowing, all-powerful Creator" what, if anything, created God?

Did you enjoy the *Wizard of Oz* as a child? Did Dorothy

believe in the Wizard, at least when she was *"...off to see the Wizard, the wonderful Wizard of Oz, because, because, because, because, because"*? As a child, did you believe that the Wizard was all-knowing and all-powerful—at least until the story revealed otherwise?

Why is there a God? Before people existed, what was God's purpose? Before life existed, what did God do?

If Humans were created no earlier than a few million years ago, what did God do for all of eternity prior to that time?

Why does God want to be worshipped? Why does God want to be feared? Might *Humans* have created this concept of a God—a deity to be feared and worshipped—in order to control and profit from other people? Can power corrupt?

Do you really need the *fear of eternal damnation* to be a good person during your life? If it were not for the threat of going to Hell, or for imprisonment for life for that matter, do you believe that you would become a criminal? How do you account for the fact that there are undoubtedly untold numbers of good-natured, loving people who are *not* Christians?

Are your religious beliefs really necessary to keep you from robbing and raping, lying and stealing, cheating and harming other people? Are you so out of control in your life that you believe that without religion you would become a menace to society?

Do you think that maybe, just possibly, the "fear of God" doesn't need to be put into you in order for you to be a good citizen? If you believe that you would become a monster without Christianity to keep you in check, what happens if Christianity turns out to be just so much out-dated hogwash? Should we lock you up *now*, before it's too late?

Is there an expiration date on God? Does God have the power to eliminate himself from existence?

Once everyone who believes in the proper creed is in Heaven with God, what will there be left for God to do? If all Humans annihilate each other through, for example, nuclear war, will life go on without us on Earth? Would universal mutual annihilation by nuclear war serve God's purposes for man? What about universal mutual annihilation by a gigantic asteroid impacting Earth—would that serve God's purposes for man? Would you welcome any such event? If God is all-powerful, why would he ever allow his Earth experiment to be terminated as to human life?

If all Humans are gone from the Earth due to any cause, will God's work be over? If all Humans on Earth die through disease, warfare or any other cause, what will God do for the remainder of the future of the Universe? Once there is no one else to save, will God simply close up shop? Will the Devil be out of work too, once there are no Humans to corrupt? Will there be wars between Heaven and Hell once there are no Humans alive?

Is Heaven a sort of after-life *Pension* for mankind? Does God administer Heaven as a trustee for the benefit of his followers? What happens if God decides to *shut Heaven down* once everyone's in Heaven who is going to be in Heaven? Can we get our money back if God goes out of business? Can believers enforce their entitlement to everlasting Heaven once they're vested (dead)?

If all Humans become extinct, but millions of years later, the Great Apes on Earth *evolve into* Humans, will God be back in business? What if God already eliminated himself from existence, will the new Humans simply live without religion? Could we do that too, starting today? In the next round of human existence, will Jesus repeat his miraculous feat of dying and resurrection, or will the first time count for the new Humans?

If you had to guess, would you guess that some kind of religious belief is probably an inevitable stage for intelligent life in the Universe as it develops into a technologically sophisticated society? Are Humans capable of living without religious beliefs? If you were a Jew, could you convert to being a Muslim? To being a Christian? To being a Hindu? To being an Atheist?

Do you believe people can recognize their mistakes and change? Even as to religious beliefs?

4. Miracles and Free Will

If we define a "miracle" as something which defies a scientific law of nature, such as a law of physics, do you believe that one or more miracles have ever occurred? Can you describe any verifiable miracle which has occurred during your lifetime? What is it?

Do you believe God could suspend the effects of gravity and make you and ten of your closest friends hover for an hour in the air a mile or so above Los Angeles against the laws of physics? Have you ever heard of this actually happening? Have you ever heard of anything remotely like this actually happening in modern times?

Do you believe that prayer can result in a miracle occurring?

Did Joshua actually pray to God that the Sun should stand still over Gideon and the Moon should stay in the valley of Ajalon? Did God cause a mighty hailstorm so that many of Joshua's enemies would die? Does God take sides in wars? Is God on your side in conflicts? Is God always on America's side?

Did the sun stand still for Joshua and his warriors against the warriors of the great city of Gideon? When Joshua prayed to God for the Sun to stand still, was the Earth flat, or was it a sphere as it is today? In order for the Sun to "stand still" for "about a whole day", did the Sun follow the Earth in its normal axial rotation or did the Earth stop rotating for a day? How did the Earth suddenly put on the brakes to stop rotating, and only for one day? How did Earth return to its normal rotation once the warriors of Gideon were defeated? Did God somehow supersede and overcome the laws of physics by stopping Earth in its tracks? Did the Sun suddenly start orbiting the Earth at breakneck speed in harmony with the Earth's rotation? How fast was the Sun moving to rotate around the Earth in a 24-hour period, considering that the average radius from Earth is eight light minutes? When the Earth suddenly slowed its rotation to a standstill (for about a whole day, as the Sun stood still in the Heavens), did everyone on Earth topple over from the massive deceleration? When the Earth decelerated to a stop, were gigantic tidal flows experienced throughout western seaboards across the globe? When the Earth started its counterclockwise rotation again, were gigantic tidal flows experienced throughout eastern seaboards across the globe? Without the normal effects of Earth's rotation on its axis and the Moon's orbit around the Earth, did devastating tsunamis result from the Sun's exceptional gravitational pull on Earth's oceans? Why weren't the various massive tidal flows and tsunami natural disasters reported in the Bible? What was the physical mechanism whereby, in the course

Miracles and Free Will

of one day, the Earth's rotation suddenly ceased and then suddenly re-commenced? Is fantasy an acceptable substitute, to you, for reality when substantiating and rationalizing your religious beliefs? Do you believe everything you read in the Bible, without question?

Do you believe that prayer can affect the likelihood of a future event happening (such as a disease being cured, or a trapped miner being rescued, or a sports game proceeding without injury)?

Do you believe that if prayers are effective in affecting the likelihood of a future event happening, prayers have this effect because of some kind of divine intervention? But if everything is predetermined, prayers must be irrelevant, correct?

May *divine intervention* defy scientific laws, such as the laws of physics? Is divine intervention a miracle?

Can all the King's horses and all the King's men ever put Humpty together again? Can God ever put Humpty together again?

Is it up to you whether or not you will pray about something? If prayer is within your control, would that mean that you have at least some input as to whether or not to pray and on what subject? That would mean that you (and not God) ultimately determines whether you pray and on what subject, correct? If God can change the future based upon your prayers, does that indicate that the future is not predetermined? But God knows everything and therefore everything has to be predetermined, isn't that right?

If everything is predetermined, how can prayers have any effect on the future? If prayers can change the future, but everything is already predetermined by God, how can prayer change the occurrence or outcome of future events? If everything is not already predetermined, then it must be true that God does not know everything, correct?

If everything in life is predetermined, is it also predetermined who will go to Heaven and who will go to Hell? Then is it true that whether a given person goes to Heaven or goes to Hell is beyond the control of that person? So God determines in advance who will believe in your church's creed and therefore who will go to Heaven, correct? If God does not know everything, then God cannot be all-powerful, isn't that right? If it is up to the individual whether he or she believes in your church's creed, then it is beyond God's control whether you'll be saved in Heaven, correct? What else is beyond God's power? Everything?

If you and another person are praying for opposite goals and your prayer is not granted, should you be thankful for God granting the other person's prayer? If you pray that the murderer of your mother is arrested before he kills again, and the killer prays that his murdering rampage continues

Miracles and Free Will

for the next twenty years, should you be thankful to God if the killer's prayer is granted by God?

If God is all-knowing, do you believe that the outcome of next Monday night's *Monday Night Football* game is predetermined? If the outcome of the game is fixed, can God be prosecuted for fixing a sporting event? Are the players who pray for a win guilty as co-conspirators?

Are competitors who pray prior to a football game ever praying for a *loss* so that the other team can experience a win? As their coach, would you encourage your team to pray for the *other* team to win? If the coach of your professional baseball team led a team prayer before every game, praying for the opposing team to win, would you pray that the coach switches teams? Would you help that idea along by firing the magnanimous coach?

As long as you are not the instrumentality of death, is it a sin to pray for your enemies to receive a free trip to Heaven as quickly as possible? Do you have anyone in mind?

Do you believe that *fatalism* (the belief that future events are predetermined and beyond your control or free will) is an unhealthy psychological state of being? Is capitalism in any way contradictory with the philosophy of fatalism?

Are you a Socialist at heart who believes that industrious people should not profit from their work? Do you believe that the dye is cast and there is no use even trying to improve your life circumstances? Should everyone get "A"s in school regardless of their level of effort and achievement? Should underprivileged children give up on trying to improve their socio-economic status?

If you believe that everything in life is predetermined, what is the purpose of society enacting and enforcing laws? What is the purpose of a free-market economy? Is real life nothing more than a pre-set game constructed by God? Are we living in a religious-themed *Matrix*?

Do you believe that Humans should be held accountable, during their lifetimes, for their actions (for example, for child molestation, rape and murder)? Are the actions of people beyond God's control? Is God a paper tiger?

On the other hand, do you believe that murderers and rapists should be *absolved* of all criminal responsibility because all events are predetermined and there is actually no free will? If the guy down the street robs you at gunpoint tonight, is that cool because it's all predetermined anyway and there is no free will?

How can God allow free will but also know what each person will do in the future ahead of time?

Are the Ten Commandments actually an early attempt by Man to enact laws to protect society from crime? Wouldn't

Miracles and Free Will

an all-knowing God create a more comprehensive set of commandments than the Ten Commandments if he really put his mind to it? Along with the Ten Commandments, did God simultaneously offer a Bill of Rights to mankind to safeguard fundamental individual *freedoms*? Is there any indication that God established a comprehensive System of Justice through Moses at Mount Sinai, including a right to jury trial, presumption of innocence, privilege against self-incrimination, right to due process of law and right to representation by counsel in any criminal investigation and prosecution?

Did God encourage freedom of speech? Did God create rules for time, place and manner exceptions to the fundamental right of freedom of speech? In ancient times, where did God speak of a One Man, One Vote concept for humanity? Did God instead tolerate and foster slavery? Did God insist upon a separation of Church and State in order to foster freedom of religion? Did Constantine's Rome violate God's Will when it fostered the one state, one religion concept?

Did God insist that Moses implement procedural and substantive due process of law? To the contrary, did God assume that he could unilaterally and without trial turn a person into a pillar of salt?

Is God merciful if he subjects all non-Christians to eternal damnation? Does God administer Justice impartially if he allows evil Christians to walk through the Pearly Gates? Are

Questioning the Word

any Christians evil? Is President Obama a Christian?

Does God *want* there to be religions which are contrary to Christianity in order that more people are destined to rot in Hell upon their deaths? Why have there been so many competing religious throughout recorded history?

Why would you twist reason and instinct to defend the concept that God's Word is *law*, if it simply does not hold up to any sophisticated analysis whatsoever? Are you a champion of *blind faith against all reason*?

Could you stand up to peer-pressure or are you the sort who joins in because all your friends do? Can you think for yourself and regularly question your basic assumptions about the viability of Christianity?

5. Souls

Really, what is a soul anyway? We all know that James Brown has soul, but why do Humans have a "soul"? Are Humans attributed with having a soul because of conceptual problems with the idea of a whole lot of human bodies over-populating Heaven? If a person's body actually went to Heaven, what would happen if it had been mutilated in battle, ravaged by leprosy or eaten by a lion? Is it easier to believe that a "soul" goes to a special place like Heaven rather than a mutilated, ravaged or consumed physical form?

After our deaths, will we be aware of our soul's individual existence? How does that happen if our brains and the rest of our body are dead?

Why do all Humans have individual souls? Why isn't there one collective soul for all Humans? Are there any Humans who missed out on getting a soul? What if God made a mistake and someone never got a soul when starting out in life?

Do you believe souls survive after death? What do our souls do while we're still living? Are souls passive or active during our lives? Do souls help us make decisions during our lives? Do our souls want us to keep living, or do our souls want us to die so that they can fully control and be in control?

Do souls communicate with other souls during our lives? Do souls have accents or speak different languages depending on where they live on Earth? Are souls filled with original sin also at our births? Do our souls sin while we're alive? Are some souls punished by being sent to Hell? Why blame our souls if they were not in control during our lives?

Is everyone's soul exactly the same, or do genetics play some role in the make-up of individual souls? Are some souls more talented, smarter, stronger, better looking or more industrious than other souls? Can souls get better with practice? Are there any schools for higher powers for souls?

Can we blame our actions in part on our guilty souls? If Humans wanted to go it alone, could they get rid of their souls during life? Can a person **actually** sell his soul to the Devil? Does the price vary according to the quality of the soul? Are all souls created equal, or are some souls substandard? Are there bargain-basement souls when it comes to the Devil's spending sprees? When the Devil negotiates a purchase of a soul, are such contracts subject to rescission for undue influence, mistake, duress or fraud? Can a sinner's soul cry foul at the precipice of Hell?

Souls

What does your soul do when you sleep? Does your soul ever communicate with you during life? What if your soul told you that God was a bad force that was a menace to humanity?

Is there any verifiable proof whatsoever that people have souls which survive their hosts' deaths? How much does a soul weigh? Can it be detected by any means? If your soul doesn't really exist, does that mean that God also doesn't exist?

Where does your soul reside while you are living? Can you lose your soul during life? Where does it go? When you become a soul, does that make you a ghost?

Are Angels and Ghosts the same thing? Do souls ever graduate to become Angels? Do Angels have souls?

Speaking of Angels, why would it be necessary for God to have physical messengers to do God's bidding? Is God hiding out? Is God's confounding mystery important to the believability of the existence of God? Did the Wizard of Oz use this same principal to continue his ruse?

Did God distinguish between Humans and all other life forms regarding souls? Why? Does it relate to the concept of **free will**?

If free will is defined as "the ability to choose between two or more alternatives in a way that cannot be predicted with certainty," do you believe that Humans have free will? Is free will important in determining why Humans have souls?

Do you believe that any life form other than Humans have souls that survive after death?

Do you believe that any life form other than Humans has free will? Have you ever owned a cat?

If other life forms, such as cats, have free will, then why would Humans have souls but no other life forms would have souls?

Is **level of intelligence** the factor used by God to distinguish between Humans and every other life form? Does a human who is brain dead at birth still get a soul from God?

If severe brain damage at birth prevents a man from ever understanding your church creed, will he go to Heaven upon his death?

Since cats and whales presumably cannot understand your church's core beliefs, are they exempt from the human prerequisites of belief? Do cats and whales have a Get-out-of-Hell-free card?

Do you believe that all life forms (for example, grass, fungus, lizards, leopards and roses) may have souls which survive death?

Souls

Are there fungi souls in Heaven? Are any of the fungi-souls shaped like mushrooms? Do they make a tasty soup?

Where is a soul prior to coming into existence? When does a new soul come into existence?

How could it have been a sin, in 2009, for a male prostitute to wear a condom to prevent the spread of HIV and **not** a sin, in 2010, for a male prostitute to wear a condom to prevent the spread of HIV? Do Humans dictate God's Word? Does God change his mind? Is God a man, a woman, or something else? Why would God change his mind if God never makes a mistake? Can we decide that God is wrong about something, and act accordingly?

Is it a sin for a man to wear a condom so as to prevent life from the imminent fertilization of the woman's egg?

Does a woman's unfertilized egg have a soul?

Does every sperm of every man's semen have an individual soul?

Are all the dead sperm souls waiting for us in Heaven?

Do you believe that before you were born, you lived in some other form of life?

Do you believe that anyone lived in some other form of life

prior to being born? Could you have been a tomato before being you? Where was your soul when you were a tomato?

What if your parents had met other people and never had children together, would your soul belong to someone else? If you were never born, what would have become of your soul? Did you take someone else's soul because your father didn't sleep around and didn't have children out of wedlock?

If you had been born from one of your current parents and somebody other than your other current parent, would you still be you? Would you have a different soul? Does which soul you have depend on who your parents are? If the identity of your soul does not depend in any way upon your heritage, what makes your soul different from any other soul? Are all souls alike in every way? Does God favor utter conformity? Why isn't there simply one soul for all Humans?

Will all "intelligent" life in other solar systems abruptly terminate once all human souls are in Heaven? Will there be ET souls in Heaven too? If there is one soul for everyone, will your soul be despondent when it's up in Heaven all alone?

In the afterlife, is all individuality lost? Is Heaven a Socialist environment? Are all colors combined to create black in Heaven? Is all interaction missing in Heaven? Are all relationships lacking in Heaven? Does anyone have fun

Souls

doing their own thing in Heaven? Is Heaven really a place of milk and honey? Can you go fishing in Heaven if you want to? What about golf? Picking tulips? Playing electric guitar?

Are the souls of siblings related? Is your soul genetically related to either of your parents' souls? Is blood thicker than water even as to souls, or is there no family loyalty after death?

Is there such a thing as an "old soul"? What does that mean?

Are old souls and nouveau riche in conflict?

6. *Evolution of Life*

Have you heard of Charles Darwin?

Do you know when Charles Darwin's The Origin of Species was published? When was it published?

Did you know that Charles Darwin was a Christian throughout his lifetime? Does that surprise you?

Do you believe that any life forms other than Humans developed from earlier life forms? For example, do you believe that whales, a marine mammal, evolved from some land mammal?

Why would other life forms **evolve** but Humans **not** evolve?

Do you believe that when Humans first walked on Earth they were generally as tall and strong as present-day Humans?

Do you believe that racial differences in Humans happened by accident? Did racial differences happen by magic? Did God arbitrarily assign various racial traits to people across the globe?

When you hear about the skeletal remains of earlier versions of Humans having been unearthed, do you think it's all a trick to mislead you from your religious beliefs?

Do you believe that live dinosaurs (of the Jurassic Park kind) and live Humans co-existed on Earth at any time in the Earth's history? Have you watched too many reruns of The Flintstones animated television show? Have Homo Sapiens existed for over 100 million years? Were dinosaurs in existence as recently as a million years ago? Did dinosaurs roam the earth 5,000 years ago? How do you know when dinosaurs roamed the earth?

Do you believe that human beings, as we know them today, developed from the Great Apes?

Why do marine mammals, such as whales, porpoises and seals, breathe oxygen through lungs, whereas fish get oxygen through gills? Slightly off topic: do you know how fish consume water?

Why do animals which live on land breathe oxygen through their lungs and not get oxygen through gills?

Why don't snakes have legs? Did snakes evolve from lizards and become more and more effective in successive generations in burrowing with ever smaller and less obtrusive legs?

QUESTIONING THE WORD

Did some dinosaurs have feathers? Are birds of today the descendants of some dinosaurs? Why do birds of a feather flock together?

Are you lactose tolerant, or lactose intolerant? Do you believe that lactose tolerance may have been an evolved human condition? Which came first: lactose tolerant Humans or lactose intolerant Humans? Why?

Do you believe that sickle cell anaemia ("SCA") may have been an evolved human condition? Does a person with SCA carry a selective advantage in exhibiting less severe symptoms if beset by malaria?

Do you believe that the ability of light-colored skin to create more Vitamin D from ultraviolet light may explain why Humans with light-colored skin thrived in far Northern and far Southern regions of Earth?

Is all life, including Humans, ancestors of single cell organisms? Did the extinction of dinosaurs pave the way for the success of small mammals?

Are Humans the only living species in the Homo genus of bipedal primates in the family Hominidae? Do Humans and the Great Apes, such as chimpanzees, both have opposable thumbs, a lack of external tails, and a similar arrangement of organs and bones? Are both Humans and the Great Apes sexually dimorphic and omnivorous? Do both Humans and the Great Apes share significant blood types and are they both affected by many comparable diseases?

Did upright walking give early Humans a natural advantage over the Great Apes? Did larger and larger brains evolve in Humans to capitalize on the advantage of intelligence? Why do Humans have a prehensile tail? Why do Humans have the vestigial organ known as a vermiform appendix? Have you eaten much foliage lately?

Are Humans continuing to evolve in perceptible respects even as you read this? If Darwin was right after all and evolution is the way of life, what role in evolution did God play? Did God simply set evolution in motion? Did God send asteriods and comets hurling around the Universe to deliver the ingredients of life to planets? Once evolution was in play, was the course of life up for grabs? Was intelligent life inevitable in the Universe? Was there ever life on Mars?

7. Spirits and Superstitions

Do you believe in witches?

Do you believe in astrology or horoscopes (for example, the idea that Humans are affected by the *astrological "sign"*—Libra, Aquarius, etc.—under which they are born)?

Did you know that astrology developed long before people understood the vast discrepancies in distances from Earth among stars in the various star "formations" (such as the Big Dipper) which are visible from Earth's position in the Milky Way Galaxy?

Are you superstitious?

If you say something bad won't happen, do you ever follow up by knocking on wood, and mean it? Do you try to avoid stepping on cracks? Do you avoid black cats walking across your path? Do you say something along the lines of, "God bless you" if someone sneezes? Do you think 13 is an unlucky number? Would you rent an office on the 13th floor

Spirits and Superstitions

of an office building and feel good about it? Have you ever thrown salt over your shoulder?

Do you believe in karma? Do you try to have good karma? Do you strive to avoid a bad mojo? Do you ever wish anyone good luck? Do you have a lucky penny, sweater, jacket or hat? Do you buy lottery tickets and try to pick a lucky number from some plan, such as the birth dates of your children? When you pass by a traffic accident, do you ever tell yourself it's lucky it was not you?

Did you know that luck is an imaginary concept having absolutely nothing to do with random chance? In fact, if you feel "lucky," do you realize that it's probably a not good time to gamble? ☺

Do you believe in demons? Do you believe that people can be possessed by demons? What about ghosts—do you believe in ghosts?

What is the Holy Ghost?

What is the Holy Spirit?

How is the Holy Spirit different from God?

Why is there a Father, Son and Holy Ghost?

Before Jesus, was there only a Father, or was the Holy Ghost already around?

Questioning the Word

Did God create the Holy Ghost specifically to impregnate the Virgin Mary without her consent?

Why is God defined in terms of people and spirits? Is God a person? Does God currently have a human form? Is God male or female or both or neither? Why?

Is God everything and nothing? Do you know what hyperbole is? Is God a paradox? If God cannot be understood, is God inherently unbelievable?

Do spirits personify the unknown and unknowable? Do you often read the fine print in contracts? Do you think that some contracts have smaller type size in parts of the contract in order *to draw attention* to those parts of the contracts, or *to deter you* from reading and understanding them? Do you think that *people who want to manipulate you* make everything easy to read, see and understand, or do they try to make it relatively *difficult* for you to read, see and understand controversial subjects?

If people believe in spirits, do you think they're apt to ask fewer questions about those spirits than if they believe in, say, their Congressman? If your Congressman came to your front door at dinner time and wanted to speak with you for a while, would that be more or less frightening than if a spirit did the same thing?

Do you think that "spirits" were invented by man long

ago in order to explain some of our fears? Would you be frightened to wake up at night and see a "spirit" hovering over your bed looking down at you? What if the spirit was actually under the covers with you, could you deal with that? Do you think that knowing how people are naturally afraid of "ghosts," someone might *use* this concept as a weapon? Do you suppose that the Holy *Ghost* just might be someone's way of controlling behavior with fear tactics?

Do you enjoy the story about Ebenezer Scrooge and those confounding ghosts? Does that story motivate you to upgrade your generosity a bit? Isn't it interesting how people can learn about human nature through art?

8. *Spreading the Word*

Does it make you sad to learn that someone you know is not a Christian?

Do want to help people learn about the Christian faith? Will you go out of your way to let people know that you're a Christian and proud of that fact? Do you want to share your faith with others? Would it please you if *everyone* believed in the Christian faith?

Do you believe that it is Christianity's *manifest destiny* to strive to reach out to **every** person on Earth in order to give them the opportunity to believe in a Christian creed?

Do you recall the Spanish Inquisition—that delightful Tribunal of the Holy Office, established in 1478 by Catholic Monarchs, under the control of the Spanish Monarchy? Did you ever learn that the Tribunal forcibly interrogated and tortured Humans (primarily those who had converted to Judaism or Islam) in order to maintain Catholic orthodoxy? Do you believe that the actions undertaken by this Tribunal in the name of Christianity were an appropriate way to spread the Christian word?

How far are you willing to go to spread the Word of God? If you believe that all non-Christians will literally go to Hell upon their deaths, why would there be <u>any</u> limits whatsoever on the measures you, or your Christian institutions, should be willing to benevolently undertake in order to enable non-Christians to convert to Christianity, and to enable Christians to remain Christians? After all, you'll be saving souls *for eternity* if you can convert them to Christianity by *any means necessary* before their deaths, correct?

Are you willing to serve the Lord through terrorist acts if necessary? Would you use fear tactics of any kind to induce another person to believe in your church's Christian creed? What if suicide bombing would terrorize some people into belief in Christian principles, would you resort to terrorism to save souls?

Would God ever ask a believer to commit a terrorist act? Is God Himself a terrorist? Is it wrong for any religion to sell itself through fear tactics? Does the notion of eternal damnation strike you as a form of religious terrorism? Have you ever told anyone that people who don't believe in Christian principles go to Hell?

Do you believe it is wrong for a Muslim believer to use any means necessary in promoting his faith? Should a Muslim use any means necessary to convert every person on Earth to belief in the Quran according to his sect?

Do you condone beheadings by ISIS to promote Islam? Do you believe that a terrorist's commitment to use any means necessary to advance their political or religious beliefs can *ever* be an acceptable methodology?

Do you suppose that some alien creatures may some day arrive on Earth with a purpose of imposing *their* strongly held religious beliefs on all of humanity? How would you feel about that?

Do you believe it was right for Moses and his Levite followers at Mount Sinai to *slaughter* all men, women and children nonbelievers who worshipped the Golden Calf? Extra credit: Do you think that Moses may have had a hand in personally creating the stone tablet *Ten Commandments* over two periods of forty days and forty nights? Alternatively, do you think that this Moses story is pure and simple fiction?

Should God have helped Joshua defeat the warriors of Gideon? Did the Lord's devastating hail storm also kill innocent men, women and children in the process? Is it acceptable for *God* to use terrorism, but not acceptable for God's *followers* to use terrorism?

Are holy wars ever truly holy? If there is no God, how wrong is it for Christians to attempt to exert their will over nonbelievers? Very wrong, or very *very* wrong?

9. The Literal Truth

Do you believe that God dictated the Bible scriptures verbatim to its authors? Do you believe *quotations* attributed to God in the Bible actually reveal direct, verbatim communications by God to the authors of the Bible?

Do you believe that God dictated the Bible *verbally* or in some other manner, such as extra-sensory perception (ESP)? Could other people hear Him when God spoke with the disciples?

If God can etch the Ten Commandments into stone, why couldn't he simply have written the scriptures of the Bible *himself*, without the disciples as middlemen?

Do you believe that God dictated *conflicting* versions of events depicted in the Bible to different persons? Why would God dictate conflicting versions of events to different persons? Was God trying to mislead Humans by misinforming them about historical events? Are there parts of the Bible which do not depict *actual historical events*?

Do you believe that God preferred to dictate the Bible to *men*, as opposed to women? Why? Is God a chauvinist? Are you aware of the quote from the Christian scholar Tertullian in *On the Dress of Women*,

> "You women are the Devil's gateway.
> You are she who persuaded Adam, whom
> the Devil did not dare attack, to partake of
> the apple. Do you not know that every one
> of you is an Eve? The sentence of God on
> your sex, lives on in this age; the guilt,
> of necessity, lives on too."?

Do you believe that the Bible as currently translated and transcribed contains no errors from the fundamental original dictates of God?

Do you believe there were any errors in transcription or interpretation from the words of God which were dictated to the authors of the Bible? What are some of these errors?

Can you describe why God chose *that particular period of time in history* to dictate his Word for the creation of a Bible? Did God close the book on the Bible?

Why did God stop dictating his words for inclusion within the Bible? Has God recently been dictating anything for any revisions or updates of the Bible?

The Literal Truth

Do you believe that everything written in the Old Testament of the Bible is literally the historical truth?

Do you believe that everything written in the New Testament of the Bible is literally the historical truth?

Did all of the dictates of God find their way into the Bible as we know it today? Are there some important scriptures which somehow were *omitted* from the Bible?

Did Emperor Constantine and thugs from the Roman Catholic Church burn books and murder anyone who was not a literalist Christian believer? Have you ever heard of the Gnostic Gospels? Does the tag "Nag Hammadi Books" ring any bells?

Do you believe that representatives of the Roman Catholic Church (such as Irenaeus) may have *fabricated* any portion of the New Testament? Have you read that Irenaeus revised the *Acts of Thomas*, renaming them the *Acts of the Apostles*? Do you know that there, Irenaeus added content confirming the historical existence of the disciples and legitimizing the Bishops by affirming their lineage from apostles? Speaking of lineage, do the Bible's *Gospel of Matthew* and *Gospel of Luke* render *wildly conflicting accounts* of Jesus' ancestral lineage? *How could that be?*

Are you aware that scholars now believe that Irenaeus created, from whole cloth, the *Pastoral Letters of Paul* in order to ascribe to Apostle Paul a purported *personal experience in the physical presence of Christ*? Could the "doubting Thomas" have had *real reason* to doubt the existence of Christ?

Did Irenaeus intercede to assure that all Gnostic Gospels, including *The Gospel of Thomas*, *The Shepherd of Hermas*, the *Gospel of the Hebrews*, and any others which deny the actual existence of Jesus, were excluded from the New Testament?

Why did Irenaeus initiate a *proclamation* that no one but Bishops, Deacons and Priests may read this New Testament? Was he wary of widespread scrutiny outside the institutional ranks?

If the last words of Christ when he was supposedly dying on the cross are reported quite differently in three Gospels, how can we trust anything reported in the Bible as being the word of God?

Would it *matter* to you if someone had altered, forged, fabricated or omitted important scriptures intended for inclusion in the Bible?

10. God's Word to Man

Do you believe that in **present** times God ever speaks to any Humans?

Have you perceived God communicating directly to you?

How often does God communicate directly to you? How do you distinguish God's direct communications from simply *thinking to yourself*? Do you ever think to yourself? If you ever think to yourself, could that actually be God talking to you?

If I ask you to think to yourself, "hippopotamus" and you then think to yourself "hippopotamus," is that God speaking to you, or is it you thinking to yourself? If it's God speaking, does that mean that I speak for God when I ask you to think "hippopotamus"?

How do you distinguish between, on the one hand, God communicating directly to you and, on the other hand, the possibility of you experiencing *psychotic hallucinations*?

When you were young, if your mother believed you were Jesus Christ, would this have been an example of God speaking with her?

When God communicates directly to you, does God always tell the truth? If God tells you that terrorism is never justified, but tells a terrorist that terrorism is sometimes justified, to whom is God lying?

Does God work in mysterious ways? Does God's work always make people happy? Does God intentionally create **natural disasters** from time to time, such as hurricanes, tornados, Earthquakes, volcanic eruptions, tsunamis, heat waves, droughts, forest fires, blizzards, and meteors hitting Earth? Is everyone happy when these natural disasters destroy property and take the lives of their loved ones? Are you glad that an earthquake in Japan caused a nuclear catastrophe? Were you pleased when tens of thousands of people were annihilated by the 2011 tsunami hitting Japan? So, sometimes then, when God acts, it does not make everyone happy, correct?

When God *speaks* to people, does it always make everyone happy? Could God have his reasons for speaking with a rapist and encouraging him to rape a child? Could God have his reasons for telling a train conductor to text message his girlfriend, causing him to miss a red signal and resulting in the death of hundreds of innocent lives in a head-on crash with another train? Could God have his reasons for whispering in the ear of an expectant mother to, "Have that abortion after all"? Could God have his reasons for describing the *winning war plan* to the enemy so that they win a battle, resulting in the slaughter of thousands of our troops?

Can you interpret virtually *everything* good or bad that might happen as resulting from God's will? Is describing the motives of God's actions as being "mysterious" simply a cop-out for having no clue why God does anything? Is it wrong for you to struggle against the natural consequences of God's plans of bad things to occur, such as tsunamis?

Does God only encourage "good" behavior and not "bad" behavior? Is it good behavior for the United States to have attacked North Vietnam, but bad behavior for North Vietnam to have defended its sovereignty?

Does good or bad behavior sometimes depend on whose perspective is being taken? Does God *always* bless America? Does every reasonable person in the United States believe that it was *God's will* for America to have invaded Iraq?

If a man's three-year-old son hits the boy's mother in the face unexpectedly with a three-pound plastic guitar, is it good or bad for the father to spank the child? Can reasonable minds differ as to whether some action is "good" or "bad"? If reasonable minds can differ as to whether an action is good or bad, then how can it be determined whether that action is or is not God's will? Is *everything* God's will?

Why would God only encourage *good* behavior, when **God himself** openly engages in *bad* behavior through, for example, the natural disasters he causes to occur? Is there *in fact* a silver lining to every cloud?

Is it God's will when a person exercises free will? If so, *is each person "God"* when exerting their free will in a manner which affects someone else's life?

If God directed you to jump off a bridge to your death, would you do that? If God told you to step on an ant, would you do that? What if God told you to conspire with others to indoctrinate children into Christian beliefs, would you do that?

Has God ever told you to do something that you believed was morally wrong?

If God unequivocally directed you to murder an abortionist, would you do that?

If God unequivocally directed you to murder a woman about to have an abortion, and then to save the fetus, would you do that?

If God unequivocally directed you to perform an abortion to save the life of the mother, would you do that?

What if God **couldn't make up His mind** as to whether to have you murder the woman or perform the abortion, what would you do? Would you ever willingly act *without regard* to what *God* wanted?

If God unequivocally directed an abortionist to perform requested abortions to better the lives of the mothers, would you support the Lord's decision?

Do you *personally know* what direct communications the Lord has had with abortionists regarding the propriety of abortions? If God directs you to murder a particular abortionist and God directs the particular abortionist to defend himself by killing you, do you pray for yourself, pray for the abortionist or pray you never believed in God?

If you murder based on direct communications from God, should that be a **complete defense** in a prosecution for Murder?

If you murder based on direct communications from God, do you deserve whatever punishment, including possibly the death penalty, which society imposes upon you? On the other hand, why should you be punished for doing exactly what God calls on you to do?

Do you believe that Christian beliefs may justify blatant violations of society's laws?

If you were an American CIA agent and were directed by that agency to find and execute an international terrorist, would you do that?

QUESTIONING THE WORD

Will you kill for your country but not for your God? If you were a Conscientious Objector, would you kill for your God but not for your country?

Do you believe that God communicates directly with schizophrenics (persons with a form of mental illness sometimes characterized by hallucinations)? Should there still be a "Not Guilty by Reason of Insanity" defense if the schizophrenic defendant honestly believes that he was following God's instructions in killing the victim? What if the defendant was **not** insane, but did honestly believe that he was following God's instruction in killing the victim—should he be treated in Court any differently from the schizophrenic?

Do you believe that the *Devil* ever communicates directly with you?

Do you believe that all *sinful temptations* are direct communications with you by the Devil? Would God ever encourage you to sin? If either God or the Devil tells a driver who lost his brakes to swerve left or swerve right, where swerving left kills a mother and her two young children and swerving right kills a father and his two young children, which is it, God or the Devil who tells the driver which way to swerve? Which way would God tell the driver to swerve, left or right? Which way would the Devil tell the driver to swerve, right or left? Who tells the driver to hit the accelerator, kill them all and never report the accident?

What if it were a matter of National Security?

Does God not determine traffic incidents? Are some things out of God's control? What things does God not control? So does God not speak to humans on some subjects? Is it true that free will in humans can be exercised in a manner where God does not know in advance the result?

Is making an unreasonable profit a sinful temptation? Would God ever encourage you to drive such a hard bargain that it's egregiously unfair to the other side?

Is it God or the Devil who tells the Chairman of the Board of a major insurance company conglomerate to maximize profit in the sale of medical insurance, even if this practice deprives many poor families of needed medical care because they cannot afford to buy the insurance?

If a church asked for an annual contribution from a church member's yearly income equal to what the member pays in State income tax, could that request be the result of a sinful temptation from the Devil to the church fathers?

If an evangelist used razzle-dazzle fear tactics to ask for donations of more than its Congregation could reasonably afford to donate, would that be the result of a sinful temptation from the Devil to the evangelist? Should everyone give most of their money to evangelists?

If a snake oil salesman convinces someone to spend money

on a worthless product, do you believe that the salesman is wrong for false advertising, the buyer is wrong for being foolish enough to buy the product, or the local Sheriff was probably paid off by the snake oil salesman?

If a *bad motive* is the key ingredient of a sinful temptation, are sinful temptations arguably everywhere? If a person smiles casually at a baby, could that be evidence of a sinful temptation? Did the Devil encourage that smile for an evil purpose? Are good intentions always subject to hypothetical criticism as being, in actuality, a veil for bad intentions? Is it always the Devil, or can it simply be a person's exercise of free will, that creates a bad motive? What if someone commits an egregious violent felony for *good* motives, is that okay?

Is it always the Devil that presents you with sinful temptations? Do people really need a "Devil" in order to be tempted by "bad" motives, or are people fully capable of exercising free will in anti-social or criminal *Malum in se* behavior?

Why did the Bible dictate that children should always submit to the authority of their parents, even if the parents' conduct was clearly misguided and harmful to the child?

Is an eye for an eye the moral equivalent of the Golden Rule? Should you do unto others as they do unto you? When gang killings are rationalized as retaliation for an earlier killing, is that the eye for an eye the Bible recommends?

Were any of the Apostles gay who wrote the words of God into the scriptures?

Is sexual desire inherent and instinctive in Humans? Do you believe that God has dictated that homosexuality (or bi-sexuality, for that matter) is sinful? If so, why did God create irreversible genetic homosexuality in some three to five percent or so of Humans?

Do you believe that without exception every homosexual is *lying* who earnestly reports that his or her sexual preference is not a matter of choice but a matter of their natural instincts?

Are the religious beliefs of Judaism any less valid than Christianity? Why?

What about the religious beliefs of Islam—are they any less valid than Christianity? Buddhism? Indian rituals? African tribal beliefs? Devil-worshipping cults? This is a free country, right? Do Christians have a God-given right to delude themselves?

11. A Woman's Place

Do you believe that Eve, then Adam, introduced original sin into the world of Humans when each took a bite of an apple?

Why do people say "Adam and Eve" and not "Eve and Adam"? Do you believe women are the root of all evil? Do you believe men are the root of all evil? Do you believe God is the root of all evil for putting original sin in mankind? Do you believe that the Devil caused God to put original sin in mankind? How could the Devil cause God to do anything?

Do you believe that women are less qualified to serve the Lord in the eyes of God?

Do you believe that in the eyes of God, women should serve the Lord in fundamentally different ways than men? Do you believe that women should serve men and that men should serve the Lord? Do you believe that femdom is a sort of feminine hygiene product? Does God bless a dominatrix? Should God be sued for unlawful discrimination based on gender?

Do you believe the world would be a better place if women were in control? Do you relish the differences between masculinity and femininity? Does God want women to be ladies in the parlor and whores in the bedroom? Does God take a position regarding human sexuality? What position does God prefer?

Did God ever choose women to write scriptures intended for the Bible? Why or why not?

If the story of Adam and Eve is not literally true, then could it be that none of the Bible is literally true?

Do the Scriptures of the Bible appear to contain an obvious and blatant gender-bias against women? Is this because of the culture of the times in which the scriptures were written by the Disciples (men)?

If the Scriptures are the Word of God why would God tell the authors to demean women in the Bible through gender-bias? If God is truly the Voice of the Bible, wouldn't God place more value on women as leaders, heads of household, Disciples and in general, equals of men?

12. Adam and Eve

Do you believe that the first two Humans to live on Earth were Adam and Eve, as described in the Old Testament of the Bible? Would Adam and Eve have been immortal had they not eaten the forbidden fruit?

If God is all-powerful and all-knowing, why would God create people (Adam and Eve) who were imperfect and who would succumb to temptation?

Did Adam and Eve start in the Garden of Eden and then come to Earth or was the Garden of Eden already on Earth at the time?

Why did an evil angel pick the snake as his or her representative in the Garden of Eden? Had the snake chosen by the evil angel in the Garden of Eden already evolved from lizards? Should Humans kill all snakes? Should Humans kill all lizards? Was the snake forgiven by God? Did the snake go to Hell? For that matter, did anyone or anything go to Hell during the period of time represented by the Old Testament? Where did people go when they died, if they died prior to the New Testament? Are they or their souls still there?

Why don't Jews believe in the concept of Hell? Is it because there is no mention whatsoever of eternal damnation or Hell in the Old Testament (also known as the Torah)?

Why did God create a Hell after the birth of Christ? Was God *playing it by ear* prior to sending his Son down to die for your sins? What was *so momentous in history* that prompted God, at that point in time, to create the Christ events and follow it up by establishing Hell?

Were Adam and Eve forgiven for their sin of eating the forbidden fruit from the tree of knowledge and then, as described in the Quran, sent down to Earth as God's representatives? Why didn't God want Adam and Eve to have knowledge? Do religions naturally tend to discourage secular education?

Did Adam and Eve simply appear on Earth as adults in an instant as inferred in the Quran, or was Adam created on Earth from dust as described in the Torah?

How can dust form a person? Can complex life be created out of dust? If God could do anything, why did God use *dust* to create Adam; why not from *nothing*? If it were **clay** and not dust, would *that* explain it?

Questioning the Word

If God took clay from many parts of the world to make Adam, that would account for the various racial types on Earth, correct? How exactly would that work? Because of the *clay differences*, did Adam's children and grandchildren start popping out with different racial features, colors and sizes? Did those races then multiply somehow and spread throughout the Earth—*particular races to particular regions* the globe (or *pancake* at that time)? Why would different kinds of clay from different geographical regions of the Earth, create different looking races?

Why would those different races disburse to different specific regions of the Earth? Did Eskimos know that their shape would be well-suited to the cold? Did Thai people understand that they could adapt well to the tropics, farming rice? Did Norwegians realize that their light skin would be well suited to sun-deprived high-latitudes in the Northern Hemisphere? Did blacks inherently grasp the advantages of dark skin and black curly hair in Africa? Did the ancients write down any of these incredible jumps of insights for posterity? Did any ethnicities ever migrate, in ancient times, to a geographical area which was *inappropriate* for their physical characteristics?

Since *liquid water* is essential to all life as we know it, why not make Adam out of water? Was Eve actually created from Adam's rib? Do you believe in the popular misconception that men have one fewer rib than women?

Before Eve was created to keep Adam company, was Adam

initially created as a hermaphrodite (both sexes as one)? Did God change Adam from a hermaphrodite into a man after Eve was created? Why didn't God *anticipate* that Adam would *want* a companion?

Since neither Adam nor Eve was born as infants from a mother, neither would have been born with umbilical cords, correct? On what day were belly buttons created?

If Adam and Eve had no childhood, how did they know how to communicate with each other? What *language* did they speak, if any? Did Adam and Eve exist before or after Stone Age Humans? How did an entire population manage to arise from two persons, considering that Adam and Eve apparently had no experience whatsoever in hunting, gathering, defending themselves, or providing shelter for themselves?

Did Adam live to be over 900 years old? Really? **700** may seem feasible, but *over* 900? Before modern medicine, why did people live to be so old? Did they find the Fountain of Youth? Should we abandon modern medicine and all move to Mount Sinai? Should you eat more seaweed?

Is belief in the literal Adam and Eve story part of the creed of your church? Do you teach that story to your children or close friends as being true? If God **lied** to his prophets, was that a sin? If you lie to your children about the origins of existence, is *that* also reprehensible?

Do you think of Adam and Eve, Santa Claus and the Easter Bunny as being in a similar, fictional, context?

If you believe that Adam and Eve were the first two Humans on Earth, and if you don't buy into the different-clay-types explanation, then how do you explain the development, over time, of the various distinct races? When in history did the various races of persons occur on Earth? Is proof of **human evolution** all around you?

Did Adam and Eve precede the Zhenpiyan culture in China, which reportedly existed in 7,600 BC? Are you aware that analysis of Chinese rice residues have been Carbon-14 dated to the Pengtoushan culture era of 8,000 to 800 BCE? Did Adam and Eve precede the Xia Dynasty in China? Did Adam and Eve precede Peking Man who reportedly lived in approximately *400,000 BC*?

Did the authors of the Bible enjoy Chinese cuisine? Where does kung fu fit in to the Bible experience? Why were the authors of the Bible oblivious to Chinese history and culture? If God knows everything, how was it possible for the authors of the Bible to not have known about Chinese history and culture? Was God *hiding* Asia from the authors of the Biblical scriptures? Why?

If you believe that Adam and Eve were the first two Humans on Earth, then did their children have incestuous unions to produce the first grand children?

Adam and Eve

At what point in history did incest become unacceptable, and why?

What if Eve had been a lesbian, or if Adam had been gay, would God's plan for procreation have been foiled?

How old was Eve when she was first created by God? What was the Age of Consent when Adam and Eve were created? Could Adam have been prosecuted for Statutory Rape under current law in the United States? Does an Age of Consent law of 16 years of age violate God's will?

Did Adam and Eve have recreational sex, unrelated to bearing children? Who performed the wedding ceremony for Adam and Eve, or did they live as an unmarried couple, in sin?

Did Adam ever masturbate? Was he properly circumcised as later dictated by God? Was circumcision part of Adam's punishment for succumbing to temptation in the Garden of Eden? Or did God enforce the rule of circumcision only later?

Did Adam ever bring Eve to an orgasm?

Are there any good Christian couples who never intend to get married but commonly engage in sex between themselves? Should they be ostracized from the church for their evil sexual union?

Questioning the Word

Is recreational sex morally wrong? Did God dictate to Adam and Eve as to what was acceptable in sexual relations?

Did The Doors' *Touch Me* song try to change residual Puritan attitudes about sex? Was Hugh Hefner's **Playboy Magazine** important in the fight against preconceptions against sexuality? Why do so many countries in the world presently have more tolerance for sexual expression than the United States? On what basis has Christianity been used, over hundreds of years, as a rally for "decency"? Was *Oh, Calcutta!* considered hopelessly indecent when it opened on Broadway in the mid-1960s? How did *Oh, Calcutta* become a tremendous and long-running (22 years!) hit?

Do acceptable levels and manners of sexual expression **change over time**? If God is all-knowing, why would concepts of acceptable moral behavior *ever* change?

Did God instruct Adam and Eve all about Christianity? Were Adam and Eve prophets in God's faith? Are there any scriptures authorized by Adam? Is there a lost Gospel of Eve?

What was Adam's last name? What was Eve's maiden name? Who were their respective parents? How did family names originate? Why doesn't anything about Adam and Eve add up?

13. Fundamental Rights

Do you believe that the United States Constitution, the Bill of Rights and the States' various Constitutions are important in establishing and maintaining liberty?

Do you believe that liberty is an admirable societal interest? Do you believe that Justice is an essential objective in a free society? Do you believe that anyone's personal religious beliefs should trump liberty and justice?

Should there be a *separation* of church and State such that religious beliefs should not be promoted by any governmental entity in the United States? Do you remember learning about the American Revolution? How did the Founding Fathers feel about historical religious persecution from Mother England?

Do you believe that Galileo was properly condemned in 1633 by the Roman Catholic Church for "vehement suspicion of heresy" for the expression of his belief that the Earth revolved around the sun, instead of the other way around?

Do you support freedom of religion as being a *fundamental right* in the United States? Do you believe freedom of religion includes the right to be an atheist or agnostic?

Would you willingly accept and respect your adult child's decision to marry and have children with an atheist or agnostic?

Do you believe that it is ethical for an atheist or agnostic to excommunicate a family member from the family for their Christian views?

Do you believe that it is ethical for a church member to excommunicate a family member from the family for their atheist or agnostic views?

Do you believe that Equal Protection of the laws as protected by the Fifth and Fourteenth Amendments to the U.S. Constitution (and similar constitutional guarantees in the various States' constitutions) establish important fundamental rights against government-sponsored discrimination in the United States?

Do you support the concept that Equal Protection of the laws should forbid any governmental entity in the United States from discriminating, without a compelling legal basis, on the basis of suspect classifications such as race, age, gender, sexual orientation, or religious beliefs?

Would you willingly accept and respect your adult child's decision to marry and have children with someone of another race?

If slavery were acceptable at the time when scriptures in the Bible were written, how can it be unacceptable today? Should we reinstate slavery? Are you willing to volunteer as a slave?

Why does Christianity repeatedly set itself up as being a higher power than the Constitution when it comes to abortion, religious freedom, sexual preferences, separation of church and state and equal protection of the law?

Do you believe Christians should refrain from doing business with non-Christians?

All other things being equal, would you hire a Christian lawyer over an atheist lawyer? Do you believe that the profit motive is an adequate justification for a lawyer to advertise that his is a "Christian" law firm?

Do you believe that Christians are more likely to be ethical, responsible and generous than non-Christians? Do you have many close friendships with non-Christian persons? Are you wary of non-Christians? Are you suspicious of non-Christians' morals and intentions?

Would it bother you to learn that many Muslims are wary of *Christians'* morals and intentions? Do you believe that it is simply *wrong* for Jews to discourage other Jews from associating with Arabs? Are you fed up yet with religious squabbling? Am I? What do you think?

14. Heaven and Hell

Do you have nightmares if you forget to say your prayers at night before sleeping? Do you have any animosity toward God for making you live in fear? Do you have any animosity toward your parents for causing you to believe in antiquated mumbo-jumbo? During college, if your parents continued to insist to you that there was a Santa Claus, would that have caused you concern?

Do you believe that Adam went to Hell?

Do you believe that Eve went to Hell?

Who was the first person to go to Hell?

Do you believe that all Humans went to Heaven who died before Jesus Christ was born?

Do you believe that all Humans went to Hell who died before Jesus Christ was born? What happened to Humans who died before Jesus Christ was born?

Can you describe how it was determined who went to Heaven and who went to Hell as to persons who died before Jesus Christ was born?

Why did God allow some Humans (who lived and died before Christ's birth) to go to Heaven without knowing about Jesus Christ? Why did God then switch the test for admission to Heaven for those persons living after Christ's birth? Was there a *grandfather clause* for some time after Christ's birth for those Humans from distant regions of the Earth who did not happen to hear the Christ story prior to their deaths?

Why would God sacrifice his son in order to save Humans from sin if God's *prior* system of determining who qualified for Heaven presumably worked fine for at least a few thousand years?

Do you believe that some people, or their souls, go to Hell after death?

Do you believe that some people, or their souls, go to Heaven after death?

Do you believe that Heaven and Hell are reserved for Humans, as opposed to other forms of life, such as dogs, crocodiles, parakeets or rice plants?

Have you ever owned a dog?

If dogs cannot go to Heaven, what happens if someone who goes to Heaven wants to take along his living, dead or dying dog?

Do you believe that a mass murderer, or his or her soul, can qualify for Heaven if he or she *genuinely repents* and expresses a *genuine belief in your church's creed* immediately before being executed by the State?

Do you believe that a pastor with an unremitting lifetime of continuous giving and genuine church beliefs could go to Hell if he spontaneously commits an absolutely heinous rape/murder immediately before being shot to death by police?

Is God a mass murderer? Did any of the small children who died in God's flood (about the time Noah's Ark was launched) go to Hell? Did they all go to Heaven? Is a child heading to Heaven ample justification for someone murdering that child? If I believe that murdering you would send you immediately to Heaven, is that ample justification for that homicidal act? If there is no statute of limitations on prosecutions for murder, should a Grand Jury be promptly convened concerning God's mass murder of innocent men, women and children during that flood? Since God apparently admitted to trying to rid the world of sinners as the motive for his epic flood, do you suppose the element of *premeditation* could be proved? Does a hobbyhorse have a hickory dick?

QUESTIONING THE WORD

Do you believe that every adult who does not hold your church's core creed beliefs at the moment of their death or incapacitation will go to Hell upon their death?

Do you believe that all or substantially all of the adult Jews murdered by the Hitler regime during World War II went to Hell if they didn't believe in the core beliefs of your church?

Do you believe that infant children of Muslims will go to Hell if they die immediately after childbirth?

Do you believe that adult native Africans *who have never heard* about your church's core beliefs (such as, that Jesus Christ was the son of God, died for our sins and rose again from the dead) will go to Hell upon their deaths?

If your church's creed materially conflicts with another Christian church's creed, does that mean that you believe that some faithful Christians who comply with one creed but not the other are going to Hell upon their deaths?

If Southern Baptists believe that the Adam and Eve story is literally true, does that mean that they believe that anyone not accepting the Adam and Eve story as a literal truth will go to Hell?

If you play in a softball league with Southern Baptists, how do you feel about the fact that their third baseman may believe that you will go to Hell because you do not believe that the first two persons in existence were a man and woman named Adam and Eve who were created by God from dust and one of Adam's ribs and ate an apple with the effect of creating original sin? Does it make you want to rip a line drive down the line? Is the third baseman's open opinion of your future in Hell grounds for his team to forfeit the game? If you reply to him, "Go to Hell", do you mean that *literally* as he does? Should your church begin to picket the Southern Baptist churches with signs like, "What the Hell?", "Hell is where the heart is", "Don't sell us Hell's half acre" and "No, **you** go to Hell!"?

Do you notice any similarities between God (or your church) threatening that you will *go to Hell* if you don't believe in Christ (and, parenthetically, donate to the church), and the mob threatening to kill you if you don't pay "protection" money (extortion)?

Do you believe that a Devil exists? Is the Devil simply God's way of playing "good cop, bad cop"? Is the Devil about as real as Darth Vader?

Do you believe that in present times the Devil ever takes on material form on Earth, such as in the body of a Human?

Do you believe that in present times any Humans are the manifestation of the Devil?

Do you believe that in present times any Humans are agents of the Devil?

Do you believe that the author of these questions may be a manifestation of the Devil? Do you believe that *you* could be the Devil and not know it? Are you?

Should the United States government fund a task force to develop intelligence on the workings of the Devil? Should the United States government work up a contingency plan for *infiltrating and eradicating* the Devil? If there could be a technological solution to discovering the existence and location of the Devil, should there be **private grants** to science for substantive studies to commence immediately? Are you willing to give? Would you like my mailing address?

Do you believe that the Devil could be hiding in the caves of Afghanistan? In Pakistan? Is the Devil hiding in your *mother's cupboard*? If we can search for alien communications from outer space, can we not also search for clandestine communications from the Devil?

Have you ever heard any communications from the Devil? Should we probe your mind for clues on the Devil's presence?

Do you believe Angels exist?

Do you believe that in present times any Humans are the manifestation of an Angel?

Do you believe that in present times any Humans are agents of an Angel?

Do you believe that in present times an Angel ever takes on material form on Earth, such as in the body of a Human?

Would most Angels be Democrats or Republicans?

Are most Angels men or women?

Are there child-Angels? Do child-Angels ever grow up? Do child-Angels ever grow old?

Do Angels ever become sick in any way? Alternatively, are Angels actually *machines or robots* of some kind?

Do any Angels ever die of old age? What ages are Angels? Are some Angels made so old that they are incapacitated? Do Angels ever age? What about child-Angels, do they ever age? When do child-Angels stop aging?

Do infant Angels ever grow up?

Is there age-discrimination in Heaven, where some Angels are allowed to be younger and some Angels are required to be elderly?

What is the optimum age for Angels?

Is the optimum age for male Angels older than the optimum age for female Angels? Are older male Angels attracted to younger female Angels, like on Earth?

Do child-Angels have the same rights and privileges as adult Angels?

Do Angels have any *say* over their existence, for example, as to assignments, vacations, with whom they may associate, what Humans they may help, and whether they have the option of exercising actual free will? Do Angels have any days off? Is there an Angels' union and collective bargaining unit?

Is Heaven a democracy? Is there a "One Angel, One Vote" policy?

Is Heaven a dictatorship?

Does God know best for you or is your input in Heaven desired and respected? Do Angels in Heaven exercise free will?

Are male Angels attracted physically to female Angels? Are some Angels homosexual?

Do Angels have frequent sexual relations? Has God ruled out sex among Angels? Can Angels at least masturbate? Are there other pleasures which God has also placed off-limits for Angels?

Heaven and Hell

Can Angels procreate? Does God approve of Angels procreating or is this done behind his back?

Does God ever have sex with Angels? Is there an Age of Consent in Heaven for sex with young Angels? Does the Age of Consent *vary* according to in what region of Heaven you happen to be? Is there an underground (or *inner-cloud*) industry in young-Angel porn?

Does every soul which goes to Heaven become an Angel? Do *any* souls which go to Heaven become Angels? Which souls become Angels? Why do some souls not become Angels? Is God playing favorites by promoting some but not all souls to Angel status? What were Angels before they became Angels?

Are there unlimited resources in Heaven? Is there a scarcity of anything which people want in Heaven? Does everyone in Heaven get everything they want?

What if someone in Heaven wanted someone else to get everything and everyone else to get nothing? What if someone in Heaven wanted nothing? What if someone in Heaven didn't know what he or she wanted, what would he or she get? What if someone wanted less than everyone else, but someone else also wanted less than everyone else?

Does God **dictate** what individual souls desire in Heaven? Is God a dictator? If God dictates what souls in Heaven want, then is "get" a better description than "want"? Do you want your soul to be manipulated in its interests and desires by God? Are souls simply robots? Is there two-man sand volleyball in Heaven?

Do souls in Heaven interact?

Are there ever any conflicts amongst the multitude of souls in Heaven?

Have any Angels ever fallen from Grace? What, if anything, prevents *more* Angels falling from Grace? Have any Angels fallen *for* Grace?

Are the rules of conduct in Heaven written out somehow so that all souls will have reasonable notice of those rules?

Is there a right to legal representation if someone is accused of *Falling from Grace* in Heaven? Is there a right to a trial by jury? Is there a right to confront and cross-examine your accusers? Is there a right to know what the charges are regarding your alleged fall from Grace? Who presides over the trial? Is the Judge also the Executioner? Is the Devil the prosecutor? Does God's dual role as Judge and Jailer create the appearance of bias and impropriety? Does God have a conflict of interest? Can a soul exercise a peremptory challenge against God? What about a challenge for cause? Can God be *recused* for his conflict of interest as Judge and Jailer?

Is there a right to any appeal from an adverse ruling by God? Does God ever get *reversed* on appeal? What *higher power* is above God so as to allow for an appeal of God's determination of fault?

If given the choice, would you prefer to live in a benevolent dictatorship or in a democracy? Do you secretly want to be someone's slave?

What checks and balances, if any, exist in Heaven? Is your personal Utopia a place where everything is decided for you?

15. Jesus Christ

Is the Christ in you? Is the Christ in each of us?

Do you believe that at any point in history there were "Gnostic Christians" who believed that Jesus Christ was a **metaphorical** Son of God who never actually existed on Earth? Have you heard that Gnostic Christians believed that Christ is in each of us? Do you know that Gnostic Christians and Literalist Christians held rival Christian theologies during the beginnings of Christianity?

Have you ever heard of the Nag Hammadi Books?

Do you believe that Gnostic Christians were systematically murdered by literalist Christians during the time of Emperor Constantine? Did you know that Gnostic Gospels were burned and banned in order to suppress their teachings? Have you heard that the Nag Hammadi Books were Gnostic Gospels which had been buried in earthen jars in caves in Nag Hammadi, Egypt in order to hide them from those who sought to burn all heretical materials in Constantine's era? Did you know that the Nag Hammadi Books were not unearthed until 1945?

Is anyone from the hierarchy or otherwise of your church willing to publicly debate either of the authors of *The Jesus Mysteries* concerning the truth about Jesus Christ? Has your Pastor ever even *mentioned* to your church's Congregation a book called *The Jesus Mysteries*? Is that a book that you just might want to read, despite any disapproval by organized Christian institutions? Do you have the courage of your convictions?

Do you believe that **Passion of the Christ**, produced by Mel Gibson, was a meaningful and important film?

Do you believe that a movie based on the book *The Jesus Mysteries* could be a meaningful and important film?

*Hundreds of years **prior*** to the purported birth of Jesus Christ, did certain Pagan religions (such as the religion based on Mithras) have *Christ stories* strikingly similar to that of Christianity's version of Jesus Christ? How is that possible?

Can you explain, by coincidence alone, the incredible similarities between the various Pagan religion Christ stories and the Christian religion Jesus Christ accounts? Do you suspect that the Christian Christ account might just be a deliberate rehashing of Pagan religions' Christ stories?

Do you believe that the first person to be aware of Jesus Christ was the Apostle Paul on the Road to Damascus?

Have you read that the Apostle Paul did not actually *see* Jesus Christ on the Road to Damascus, but only *heard* about him from God and saw a light?

Do you believe that the Apostle Paul conceived of Christianity as a means of providing a path to Heaven for Gentiles, where no path otherwise existed under the Torah?

Whose genes were mixed with the Virgin Mary's in order to give birth to Jesus?

Did the Holy Spirit have DNA?

Whose DNA does the Holy Spirit have (who was his mother and father)? Why was the Holy Spirit a male and not a female?

Did the Virgin Mary receive someone's semen without intercourse? Whose?

Was the Virgin Mary raped by God (or the Holy Spirit) who impregnated her without her consent? Did the Virgin Mary need counseling after giving birth without prior sexual intercourse? When the Virgin Mary insisted to friends that she had never had intercourse prior to giving birth to Christ, was she ostracized as being a crack-pot?

Jesus Christ

Did God romance the Virgin Mary prior to allowing her to be impregnated via Immaculate Conception? Could the Virgin Mary have sued God for battery and rape for being impregnated by God without her consent? Did God obtain the Virgin Mary's consent to impregnate her? Can you describe the conversation God had with the Virgin Mary in order to gain her consent for the Holy Impregnation? Did God decide that he did not need the Virgin Mary's consent to impregnate her?

Did God provide child support to the Virgin Mary for the 18 years of Christ's minority?

Was Christ rebellious in his youth? Why isn't anything revealed about Christ's childhood after the three Shepherds visited him with gifts? Did Mary write an autobiography about her lifetime achievement of giving birth to God incarnate, Jesus Christ? What have we learned from Mary about the childhood of Christ?

How did God choose the Virgin Mary as the mother of Christ? Was there an interview process? Were other prospective mothers of Christ interviewed and considered? Did the word get out that God was in the market for a mother to his child? Were other applicants turned down because, for example, they preferred a daughter to a son?

Why did God send down his son and not his daughter to save Humans?

Did God ever have more than one child? Why or why not? Did the Holy Ghost have sex out of wedlock?

How many children did Jesus father? Is there anything inherently wrong about a couple consensually engaging in sex without a formal marital decree? If it's true that Jesus was both the Son of God and human, did Jesus ever have sex with a woman of child-bearing age? Was Jesus gay? Was he infertile? Did Jesus masturbate regularly?

If Jesus was such an incredibly important historical figure, why wasn't there anything substantive written about his "life" until at least 30 to 50 years after his death? How could such an event as *the entire life and death of Christ* go unreported for so long?

Do you believe that Jesus will return to Earth for "rapture" in order to murder all then-living Humans, such that all who have been saved will go with Jesus up to Heaven and all who have no faith in Jesus will not be saved?

Do you have any idea when the rapture event will occur? Will you send a Tweet letting us know at least 24 hours in advance?

Why hasn't the rapture event occurred after all these centuries since the time of Christ's life/death/life?

Should still another Grand Jury be convened seeking a

criminal indictment of Christ for *conspiring* to conduct a terrorist act—to wit: the rapture? Is the element of an overt act missing in this conspiracy to date?

If you believe that rapture will occur within the next five years, is it wrong for you to take out a twenty-year mortgage on your house, knowing that you may not need to pay fifteen years of your debt? If rapture will occur within the next five years, should this be a defensible tax basis for accelerating depreciation on an office building?

16. The Creation Story

Did the six days of creation as described in the Bible occur in strict chronological order?

Was God working on the basis of an Earth-day, or is a day a day no matter where you are? Did each day of the six days of creation cover a 24 hour period of time? How many hours in a moon-day? (Is that a trick question?) How many hours are there in a Mars-day? What about a Jupiter-day or Mercury-day?

What is the firmament of Earth? Do you believe that presently, part of the seas are "under the firmament", as they were on the second day? Is Nevada floating on water?

On which of the first six days were viruses created?

On which of the first six days were dinosaurs created?

After Adam and Eve set foot on terra firma, when did dinosaurs become extinct?

The Creation Story

Were Neanderthals in existence before or after Adam and Eve? How did Neanderthals come into existence? Where does the Bible speak of Neanderthals? If Neanderthals disappeared as a human subspecies around 28,000 years ago, how many years ago were Adam and Eve created by God? Why did Neanderthals become extinct or subsumed into other species of Humans? Did God make a mistake in his planning?

Was the Earth spinning once every approximately 24 hours when it was created, so as to create the 24-hour period of a single day? How does the Bible describe that the Earth rotates on its axis? Was the earth flat during the era of Adam and Eve?

If God created light on the first day, but did not create the sun until the third day, what was the source of the light on Earth for the first two days?

Before the sun ("the greater light to rule the day") was created, how did the *darkness* fall over Earth? When did darkness fall over Earth? When Earth was first created, how was it determined that a day had elapsed, since (except for the effects of eclipses) lightness and darkness are applicable to a planet only if that planet is rotating relative to a source of light?

If God made the Earth **prior** to creating the sun, was the Earth *in orbit* before the sun was created? What exactly did the Earth *orbit* before the sun was created? In the beginning, did Earth defy the laws of physics and orbit nothing in particular?

What started the Earth to orbit the sun? Did God give it a little push?

What do apples falling from a tree and tidal flows have in common?

Why would God create life only on Earth? Why did God pick Earth, of all places, for his experiment with Humans? How lucky is that for Christians? Is Earth still the center of the Universe, even centuries after the works of Copernicus, Kepler and Galileo?

If a UFO landed and alien beings stepped off onto the Santa Monica pier to look around, would this change your opinion of whether God created life *only* on Earth?

Is God's Creation story for every *other* planet with intelligent life in the Universe *consistent* with the Creation story for Earth found in the Bible?

Did God create other planets that orbited the sun during the first six days of creation? Why did God create other planets to orbit the sun? How do the other planets work into God's plan for Humans on Earth? When was the planet Mars created by God? Why isn't the gas-giant Saturn specifically mentioned in the Bible?

The Creation Story

During the first six days of creation, did God create planets which orbited any stars other than the sun? When did God create the planets which we now know to orbit other stars in the Universe? Why isn't this documented by the scriptures within the Bible? Since God knows all, he knew about planets when he vicariously authored the Bible, correct?

Is the Bible interesting, if only as a well-preserved *time capsule*, as to ancient and antiquated thinking, knowledge and life-concepts?

Do you believe that probably there is some intelligent life on planets other than Earth somewhere in the Universe? Were all planets with intelligent life, including Earth, created **simultaneously** with the Heavens and the Earth?

How do you explain the *proven* scientific fact that while Earth's solar system is approximately 5 billion years old, other stars, planets and galaxies were created billions of years before? Does that mean that parts of the "Heavens" were created billions of years **before** the Earth, and that therefore the "Heavens and the Earth" were *not* created simultaneously as indicated in the Bible?

If some of the galaxies we have observed are some **13.7 billion** "look-back" *light years* away from Earth, how could the light from those galaxies reach Earth in only 5,000 years?

Why did God refer to the sun as "the greater light" and other stars simply as "stars"? Did God forget that the sun is simply another star? Was God trying to mislead man into believing that the sun was something *qualitatively different* than other stars?

Why did God create whales and creeping things before making "man in our image, after our likeness"?

If Humans are in the likeness of God, does that mean that giraffes are *not* in the likeness of God?

Why doesn't God want giraffes to have everlasting life? Do giraffes have original sin? Should good Christians not allow their children to play with toy giraffes? Are giraffes the manifestation of evil and undeserving of entry into Heaven?

How are Humans in the likeness of God? How can Humans be in the likeness of God if we are inherently sinners? Is God an itinerant sinner?

Are any life forms elsewhere in the Universe also in the likeness of God?

Will all technologically savvy species look just like us, as in the likeness of God?

Why did God grant Humans "*dominion* over the fish of the sea, and over the fowl of the air, and over every living thing that moveth upon the Earth"? Doesn't God believe in conservation? Is it alright after all to serve shark-fin soup?

If God is all-knowing, then why did he dictate for the Bible an historical account of the origins of the universe that is so at odds with actual laws and factual discoveries of science which are commonly accepted today? Why doesn't the Bible at least conform to modern concepts of common sense? Does the story of Noah's Ark ring true to you as an actual account of historical events? Really?

17. Noah's Ark

Do you believe that Noah actually took two to seven of every air-breathing creature on his Ark to save them from the impending world flood? When, in the course of the past 5,000 years, did the Noah's Ark event take place?

Was God justified in causing a rain of forty days and forty nights for the purpose of murdering every air-breathing living thing on Earth (including people) except for those which/who made it on board the Ark? Why did God make reindeer responsible for the sins of humans? On the other hand, why did God spare fish in his murderous flood rampage? Should God have poisoned all of the fish and marine animals except those invited to live in an aquarium on board the Ark? God did have the technology to assist Noah in creating a massive on-board aquarium, correct? Speaking of air-breathing creatures, did God put pilot whales, blue whales, porpoises, seals, walruses, sea lions, sea otters, sea snakes, turtles and hump back whales—all air-breathing marine creatures—into an onboard aquarium on the Ark? How did grey whales, sperm whales and Killer whales get along in the Ark's aquarium?

Did the flood cover the Himalayas, including Mount Everest? Where did all this water come from to raise sea level so high throughout the world? Did ice flows and glaciers melt away to pave the way? Did we have a new Ice Age after that which has never been discovered by scientists?

When the rains subsided, to what location did the flood waters recede? Does Earth have a giant storm drain somewhere for 40 days and 40 nights of flood waters? Would that be known as the 5,000-year storm drain system?

What transgressions, of mankind as a whole, could *possibly have justified* God killing all air-breathing life on Earth except for what made it onto the Ark? Is a mass murder of innocent men, women, children and giraffes justified by *any* religious dogma? Does God's flood make 9/11 look like child's play?

Were terrorists justified after all in their 9/11 acts of violence? Is the God who designed and implemented the murderous flood—*God the Terrorist*—the God you worship? What did God **accomplish** with his ultimate act of terror against the life on Earth? After the flood, was mankind any less inclined to engage in sexual relations? After the flood, was mankind any less inclined toward violence? After the flood, did theft and deception end for all time? Did God make yet another mistake? If God is all-knowing, why didn't he know that his world flood and Noah-move would accomplish *no positive end results*?

Did Noah take two to seven of every species of bird with him on the Ark?

Did Noah take two to seven of every penguin with him on the Ark?

Did Noah take two to seven Grizzly bears with him on the Ark?

If Noah took two to seven rats with him on the Ark (for forty days and forty nights plus 150 days of flood), how many rats were there on the Ark when the flood receded?

Did Noah take two to seven Komodo Dragons with him on the Ark? Did anything or anyone die from being bitten?

Did Noah take two to seven of every breed of elephant with him on the Ark? How did the African elephants get along with the Indian elephants?

Did Noah take two to seven woolly mammoths with him on the Ark? Sabre Toothed tigers? Dinosaurs? Why is there no reference in the Bible to dinosaurs? God must have known that dinosaurs existed at some time in Earth's history, correct? Why didn't God pass this interesting bit of prehistoric news down to man through his prophets?

Noah's Ark

Did Noah take two to seven of every species of dog with him on the Ark? Were there poodles at that time during the Great Flood? Back in the days of Noah's Ark did people trim poodles the same as now? Did the toy poodles get to wear cute knitted sweaters on cold nights during the journey of Noah's Ark?

How did wolves get along with the poodles on Noah's Ark? Did they eat the poodles? Did tigers eat the wolves? How did the Bengal tigers and African lions do together?

Did Noah take two to seven Polar bears with him on the Ark?

Did any of the Polar bears survive the uncommonly warm weather and lack of ice? Where are Polar bears mentioned in the Bible?

Did Noah take two to seven Chinese panda bears with him on the Ark?

Did Noah take two to seven African crocodiles with him on the Ark? Did the crocodiles ever get loose and rip any of the other animals or people to shreds on the Ark? Which animals or people were ripped to shreds by crocodiles?

Did the Asian crocodiles get along with the Louisiana alligators on the Ark?

Did Noah take two to seven South American boa constrictors with him on the Ark?

Did Noah take two to seven centipedes, scorpions, brown recluse spiders, black widows, every other kind of spider, Gila Monsters, black mamba snakes, rattlers, cobras, every other kind of snake, and North American Big Horn sheep with him on the Ark? Did Noah take two to seven fleas, ticks, mites and bed bugs with him on the Ark?

Did Noah take two to seven kangaroos and duck-billed platypuses from Down Under with him on the Ark? For that matter, when the flood *receded*, did Noah take the kangaroos *back* to Australia, or are kangaroos mysteriously native to *both* Australia and the Middle East?

Did Noah take with him two to seven organisms which do not need the classic male and female forms to replicate?

Did God magically cause all animals, even the wild animals, to be docile and friendly while on the Ark? If that's true, why did God separate wild animals from domesticated animals on the Ark as described in the Bible?

Did Noah take two to seven of every fresh water fish with him on the Ark?

Did all of the fresh water fish on Earth die during the flood because of the high salinity of the world flood?

Did any of the salt water marine life on Earth die in the Seas because of the high degree of fresh water dilution of salt water during the great flood?

At the time of the flood, did Noah *look* like a 700-something year old man? Is there any reference in the Bible to Noah in his *youth*, say, when he was only 300-something? If Noah was so perfect and lived over 700 years, why aren't there any references in the Bible to all his good deeds and civic achievements *prior* to the great flood?

How is it possible that among all the violence and sinfulness of mankind, Noah was *perfect* and walked with God? Did Noah ever have any evil thoughts? Did Noah ever overeat? Did Noah ever covet his neighbor's wife? Did Noah warn anyone of the impending flood disaster? Did Noah nobly ask God for permission to have *someone else* take his place on the Ark to save at least one life? Did Noah ever have an orgasm out of wedlock?

Regardless of the Biblical description of Noah, is it really possible for **anyone** to be perfect except in a fictional fantasy? Also, is it *believable* that Noah was the *only one person in the world* sufficiently honorable to deserve to be spared the wrath of God's super-flood?

Did God forever sanction *nepotism* when he spared Noah's wife, sons and daughters-in-law from the global bloodbath simply on the basis of their relationship with Noah?

QUESTIONING THE WORD

Do people want to believe in *fantasy* as a convenient replacement for reality? Is this affinity with a substitute reality one of the reasons that drug and alcohol abuse is so persistent in society?

Who were the wives of Noah's three sons whom he took with him on the Ark? Did they have names in the Noah story? Do you remember them?

After Noah and his family survived the flood, did the **practice of incest** once again take hold on Earth as the required method of procreation for Humans? When did incest again become undesirable after Noah's Ark, and why?

What did Noah take aboard the Ark to feed and provide water for all of these living things during the journey? Did Noah and his family experience scurvy during their journey on the Ark? How did they preserve their food and water?

How many of the living things ate other living things on the Ark? Which ones? Were any species *wiped out to extinction* from being eaten on the Ark by other species? Which ones? Did any of the living things on the Ark *die from disease* arising from lack of sanitary conditions on the Ark (nowhere to defecate and urinate, and no way to clean up the mess)?

Of all the untold numbers of species on Noah's Ark, how many simply died of natural causes during the journey? Which ones? How did the remaining life-form of the pair reproduce without a mate? What if some of the dead ones were females, did any of their unborn children also die while the mother was on the Ark?

Were any of the untold numbers of species on Noah's Ark *infertile* or otherwise incapable of reproducing offspring? Which ones? How did the infertile couple reproduce offspring later if one or both of the animals were infertile?

How did Noah *collect* all of these diverse species from all over the world to be saved on the Ark? Did the sailing technology exist during Noah's era necessary to accomplish his pre-flood journey?

How long did it take Noah to collect all of these species from all over the world? When Noah was collecting animals, did **he** actually discover America instead of Columbus or Chinese explorers? Should the United States cancel **Columbus Day** and celebrate **Noah's Day** instead?

Did Noah have an **expeditionary team** that helped him collect all of these species from all over the world? Is there any written record, in the Bible or otherwise, which chronicles the journey of Noah's expeditionary team around the world during its collection process?

Was it actually Noah and his expeditionary team, and not Ferdinand Magellan in 1519 to 1521, to first circumnavigate the globe? Should all history books be corrected in these regards?

What happened to Noah's expeditionary team after the Ark was launched without them during the flood? Did God throw the expeditionary team under the bus? Did the expeditionary team get to rise from the dead like Jesus?

If there was no expeditionary team collecting animals, did God instead, simply "teleport" all of the animals and creatures from around the globe to the vicinity of Noah's Ark? It works in **Star Trek**, why not for God, correct?

If the idea was to kill all the **people** except for Noah and his family, and not the animals, why didn't God simply temporarily *levitate* all of the animals, let the people drown and provide Noah a sea-going boat for him and his family? Would the story of *Noah's Boat* be less dramatically appealing than a story of *Noah's Ark*?

Speaking of boats, how many other, unauthorized people escaped God's wrath and rode out the flood in boats? Did any sailors ride out the storm in the ships? Where are their stories contained in the Bible? Could this be a subject of a popular documentary film yet to be lensed—*Harrowing Sailing Tales from the Epic World Flood*? Should Noah have written the preface to this documentary? Is there a secret society of unauthorized seafarers who slipped the proverbial noose of God's epic flood?

How **big** was Noah's Ark to hold the immense weight of two to seven of every species of animal on Earth? Could such an Ark be built with *current* technology today? Did **aliens** help

Noah with futuristic engineering technology to facilitate the construction of this incredible Ark?

Once the flooding subsided, did Noah and his family utilize the futuristic technology from the Ark's design and construction? After the flood subsided, did Noah and his family start the first engineering company in history and catapult engineering technology thousands of years into the future? Why didn't that happen?

If God wanted to murder all of the men, women and children on earth (except for Noah's family), why would he need a flood to do that? Why not a drought? A disease? Why not simply zap everyone out of existence.

Were ancient people more gullible than you? Were skeptics of these implausible stories murdered by the likes of Moses?

Would you expect that advancing technology, scientific discoveries, widespread education and the ready availability of mass media communication including, notably, the Internet, would tend over time to make people better informed, more inquisitive and less gullible? Do you *think*?

18. Life and Death

Are you afraid of death?

Do you welcome death with open arms because you are completely confident that in death you will find the Gates of Heaven open and waiting for you?

Would you walk in front of a fast-moving train tomorrow morning willingly?

If you want to be in Heaven, why not commit suicide today? In fact, why not take out as many Christians as you can with you?

Is it wrong to prolong life if death brings faster results of everlasting life?

Is the practice of medicine anti-Christian since it tends to delay death and everlasting life? Do Christian Science believers have it right after all?

If, because of God's proscription of suicide, Christians can't commit suicide, why not take matters into their *own* hands and get other Christians moving quickly toward Heaven? Couldn't they effectively absolve themselves of this sin by asking for forgiveness afterwords?

Why would God make suicide a sin (or worse yet, a "mortal" sin) if suicide would bring Humans to His side more speedily? Is it alright for God to kill Humans because they're evil and corrupt, but not alright for Humans to kill themselves because they're righteous?

Why did God create a survival instinct in Humans? If Humans have a survival instinct, is that instinct anti-Christian since it tends to delay one's journey to Heaven?

Why would God cause whales to commit suicide if he cared for them? Why would God cause a man such grief that he would take his own life? Why should suicide be viewed as sinful if the person dying has been living in hell on earth? Shouldn't God greet the poor soul with open arms?

Does your entire life boil down to being merely a test of whether you qualify for Heaven? Who authorized God to administer tests? Can God's test results be *audited* to assure accuracy and an absence of improper and inappropriate bias? Why are adults being tested against their will? Can we demand a popular vote on this testing business? Who appointed *him* God, anyway?

Questioning the Word

Alternatively, is the drive to reach Heaven all about the fear of death? Are entire industries today built upon mankind's instinctive desire for youth and immortality?

Aside from perhaps Captain Jack Sparrow and his cronies, has anyone ever discovered a fail-safe Fountain of Youth? Is religion a ready answer to the popular search for everlasting life?

Have Humans generally become more righteous since the time of the Noah's Ark incident? If so, why has God *punished* modern Humans by *shortening* their lives from hundreds of years down to an average of around 85 today?

On the other hand, if the life span of Humans has actually *increased* over the centuries, why does the Bible falsely claim that some people then lived to be *several hundred* years old?

19. Faith and Verifiable Fact

What is "faith"? Ultimately, is faith simply a belief without a shred of proof?

Do you believe that at some level of analysis, Christian beliefs eventually require "faith"?

Is the word "faith" the answer to all questions regarding the truth of your religion? Do you know what a "bootstrap" argument is? As an adult, are you satisfied with the childhood answer, "Just *because*"?

In your everyday life decisions, is **no answer** enough for you? Are your religious beliefs simply *less* important to you than everyday life issues? Would, "Have a little faith," be a sufficient final response to you if you asked why you're not being paid for this past pay-period's work? Is, "*Have a little faith, it's okay, really*." going to satisfy you?

Why do we insist upon transparency in business, our personal affairs, and government, but allow religious precepts to be shrouded in confounding mystery?

Do you believe that scientific advancement would optimally occur through "faith" in untested theories? Would you prefer to turn back the clock of scientific methodology say, five hundred years? Is astrology inherently more interesting to you than astronomy? Are you willing to give up Facebook?

Do you feel that you were born *too late*? If only you lived in the 1500s, would that be a delight? Do you privately yearn to risk merciless persecution for your religious beliefs?

If someone truly believes, by pure faith alone, that anything that he or she touches will last forever in its current form (which I will call, the "Last-Forever Faith"), will you believe that too? Could you become a True Believer in the Last-Forever Faith without any reliable proof of its validity?

Why do Christianity *and every other religious dogma* depend on *faith* and not scientifically verifiable fact? If scientists could prove religious precepts, do you think that such proof would have occurred at least to some extent by now? Is it an answer to claim that religion can neither be questioned nor proved?

If religious leaders had proof of the viability of Immaculate Conception in Humans, do you suppose it would have made front-page news?

If Angels really were *in the Outfield*, do you suppose there might be more than a comedy feature film documenting that fact?

If God were so bold, thousands of years ago, to lend his Voice to the prophets, to openly perform spectacular miracles and to send his son down to Earth to die for our sins, why, in modern times, has God avoided the spotlight?

Why are so many Humans of so many differing religious systems willing to *suspend all reason* by adopting fairy tales as their life mission statement? Are we as a species *that desperate* for a response to our innate fears? What allows one person to engage in critical thinking and leaves another person flat?

Can you think for yourself? *Do* you think for yourself? Can you buck the religious system if the system just might be… total… *falsehoods*? Can you? *Will* you?

20. Science and Religion

If light travels at a maximum speed of 300 million meters per second, could God make it travel even more quickly?

If light from the Andromeda Galaxy takes more than two million *years* to travel to Earth, did the light from that galaxy now arriving here start before or after the beginning of Earth time? What about the light from galaxies observed, photographed and studied by Edwin Hubble at about **a *thousand million* light years of distance away from Earth**—did that light start toward us before or after Adam and Eve lived on Earth?

How is it possible that our Solar System is only about five billion years old, while the Universe itself is on the order of about 13.81 billion years old?

Are all stars that we can detect through telescopes contained within our own Milky Way galaxy, or are there galaxies outside of and beyond the Milky Way?

Have Hubble Telescope images expanded our sense of the magnitude and complexity of the Universe? Have you looked at Hubble images on the Internet lately?

Does the Universe today look the same as it did billions of years before? Is the Universe unchanging? Are astrophysicists simply wrong when they point out that the Universe itself is evolving?

Over time, throughout our Universe, are new stars born and do old stars die out? Do galaxies develop and evolve over time? Why are there barred-spiral galaxies, spiral galaxies, giant elliptical galaxies and other-shaped galaxies in the Universe? Why are there galaxies at all? Did God mention the existence of galaxies to us in the Bible scriptures? Why not?

What role do galaxies play in the evolution of our Universe? Do galaxies merge and change in size and shape? Utilizing long-exposure deep space photographs, can we in effect *look back in time* and "see" galaxies forming and merging?

What in the world, if anything, could all those galaxies, energy sources and potential life forms have to do with God's plan *for Humans*? Do you believe supernatural forces affect events in the Universe? Do we really need a belief in *magic* to understand the existence and evolution of the Universe?

Questioning the Word

Considering the speed of light at 300 million meters per second, if galaxies were billions of light years away from us in space, would that interest you? Why is it important to understand the vast distances from our Milky Way to other galaxies in the Universe?

Did you know that in viewing light through powerful telescopes and long-period photographic equipment, a "redshift" (stretching the light towards the long-wave red color of the light spectrum) is revealed in the spectrum of light from all distant galaxies (except for the Local Group in which the Milky Way is a part)? What is the scientific significance of such a widespread redshift?

How is it possible for all galaxies in the Universe, except for relatively nearby galaxies, to be *simultaneously moving away* from the Milky Way galaxy? Why would there be a redshift of light from virtually every galaxy in every corner of the Universe? Could such a redshift, varying in degree from galaxy to galaxy, have been caused by a *stretching of space itself*, similar to the surface of a balloon stretching as it is blown up?

Have scientists proved beyond reasonable doubt that our Universe is expanding such that the "space" is literally *stretching* throughout the Universe? Will the expanding Universe expand forever until we can no longer see other stars in the sky and all new star formation ceases?

SCIENCE AND RELIGION

Did you know that Edwin Hubble discovered a clear and precise *mathematical correlation* (formula) between, on the one hand, the degree of observable redshift and, on the other hand, distance to the source of light, such that the distance to every galaxy can be determined by reference to Hubble's famous "redshift-distance" law?

If space is expanding—or more accurately, "stretching" —does this indicate that at some distant time in the past, the Universe *started from some very, very small space*? When the stretching began, how large was the Universe? Will the stretching ever end?

Will our Universe eventually slow its expansion to a stop and proceed to collapse upon itself, or will it continue to expand forever? In the future, if the redshifting stops and the spectrum of light from all galaxies shifts from a redshift into a *blueshift* (squeezing the light towards the short-wave blue color of the light spectrum) in the spectrum of light, what are the long-term implications? Should we run for cover?

What is the ultimate result to our Universe of such a future blueshifting event? Will Earth be long gone through the death of the Sun prior to the occurrence of this blueshifting event? Will intelligent life then be searching for a new Universe to call home?

If Earth's Solar System is actually inside of a black hole,

would the black hole's eventual collapse into a singularity be God's way of implementing his rapture event; or is this simply part of the natural evolution of universes? Is a period of time in excess of *30 billion years* what the Bible had in mind when it declared that the rapture would happen soon?

How could a collapse of the entire universe be *Earth's* rapture if within about five billion years from now our Sun will expand to a Red Giant star and obliterate the Earth in the process? Or is *that* the rapture?

If a singularity from our Universe explodes again and new life eventually forms, will the Bible be rewritten exactly as before? Does history literally repeat itself, or does God learn from his mistakes? Will there be another "Old" Testament, or will God start with a "First-Amended New" Testament this next time?

Is our Universe the first ever, or have there been previous Universes? Is our Universe presently alone or are there other, simultaneously existing, parallel universes?

Is M-Theory a recipe for M&M candies or something a bit more significant? Is it really believable today that everything and everywhere has been created *for Humans*, or are Humans simply *one form of the diversity of life* within a vast living Universe?

If, by extrapolation from X-ray studies of portions of space (and other techniques), scientists have estimated that there exist *hundreds of billions* of black holes within the Milky Way galaxy, what are the implications for the Universe as a whole? Did you know that astronomers widely believe that the Milky Way is but one of *billions* of galaxies in the known Universe? Does the existence of black holes pertain to the formation of stars and therefore to the evolution of the Universe as a whole?

Is God's work completed in other areas of the Universe where, for example, black holes and resulting supernova explosions of stars have already wiped out their life-giving planets, annihilating any and all indigenous life forms? Does the path to life begin anew from each supernova explosion, spreading complex organic molecules and shock waves throughout interstellar space?

What is life, in the biological sense? Is life something that can replicate itself and has interaction with the outside world? Is a rhinoceros alive? Are bacteria alive? Is a virus alive? What about DNA, is that independently alive?

What exactly did God *do* to create life? What could God do to create life that Nature could not have done (or did not do) *on its own*? Why are carbon, nitrogen and oxygen essential ingredients of most biological life? What is the significance, if any, of the scientific detection, **in clouds of gas in space**, of ammonia, formaldehyde, water, formic acid, methanimine and glycine? How is the discovery in deep space of *cellulose* (an essential component of plants), important in the understanding of the origins of life on Earth?

Does the interstellar production of *complex chemical compounds for billions of years prior to the birth of the Solar System* have any *importance* in gauging the chances of life developing on Earth over its five billion year history? If you think about that question once more, does it help you understand? Complex chemical compounds in the universe, produced for billions of years *before* creation of Earth—what significance could that have? (In your mind, do you hear the music playing to *Jeopardy*?)

Why would we automatically assume that life originated initially on the Sun's planet *Earth* instead of life *first originating* on a planet orbiting some *other* star **billions of years earlier**? Was life inevitable on Earth where the natural precursors of life developed throughout the Universe over some 13.81 billion years of time? Have comets from deep space seeded Earth with the essential building blocks of life for billions of years? Can you imagine that?

Are ancestors of Humans single cell organisms which in turn evolved from complex interstellar organic chemicals?

Is God superfluous to this process, or was there a "guiding hand"? What, specifically, did the guiding hand do? If a guiding hand set the forces of nature into motion, does it necessarily follow that that guiding hand also meddles in human affairs billions of years later? Is magic real, or created for the willing, uninformed and misdirected mind?

What is "gravity" anyway? How can both statements be true that: (1) nothing can travel faster than the speed of light; and (2) the speed of light is a constant? If light is emitted, from a star moving directly in our direction, how can it be possible that the light still travels only at the maximum speed of light, as opposed to the speed of light plus the closing speed of the star headed in our direction? **Are space and time** actually *interconnected*, as described in Einstein's theory of Special Relativity? Are mass and energy also interconnected, as postulated by Einstein's famous formula $E=mc^2$ (energy equals mass times the speed of light squared)? Does the *proliferation of matter* throughout the Universe cause "spacetime" *to bend* so that the Universe itself initially stretches and expands?

Did you know that the "visible" gas clouds, galaxies, stars, planets, comets and the like comprise only 1% of the mass of the entire Universe, and that the *remaining 99% of the mass of the Universe* is some "dark" matter which *exists but does not interact* with other mass *except* through gravitational effects? Is "gravity" an essential prerequisite for life? On what day of Creation did God create gravity? Does "time" slow down, relative to Earth time, on or near objects with more mass than the Earth? What is the effect of speed, relative to the Earth, on time? Is a day of Creation the same everywhere, under all circumstances, or is the entire concept of a "day" illusory with respect to time?

Would you like to understand the profound significance of the scientific confirmation/discovery that the entire Universe has microwave radiation at an average temperature of approximately 2.7 degrees above absolute zero (Kelvin)? Would you be interested to learn that ripples of non-uniformity in microwave radiation in the Universe, and corresponding variations in the exact temperature of deep space, *precisely confirm* mathematical predictions of present-day conditions following the Big Bang? Do you believe in the Big Bang Theory?

Why is the sky at night essentially dark? Is the night sky *dark* because there is an **edge** to the Universe beyond which we cannot see, or because of some other factors preventing the night sky from being a *bright* night sky?

Was the Universe always here, stretching back infinitely in time? Is the Universe infinite in three-dimensional distance? If infinite space is filled with an infinite amount of stars and galaxies existing for an infinite amount of time, wouldn't the night sky be virtually *emblazoned* with light, as if in a room illuminated by densely packed ceiling lights? If the Universe is unchanging and all of the light from an infinite number of galaxies has been unchanging for an infinite amount of time, wouldn't we see all that light in every space of a night sky?

On the other hand, if the Universe actually came into existence only some 13.81 billion years ago with a finite amount of visible mass, what implication does that entail about why the night sky is only a starry sky and not *brilliantly* bright? Is this the reason why the night sky is not completely filled with an infinite amount of starlight? Does the obvious fact of a dark, starry night sky tend to prove that the Universe had a finite beginning in time, albeit a long, long time ago?

Why are planets *planets*, and stars *stars*? Is this magic? Is it a supernatural event? Is it completely random and arbitrary? Did God create stars and in effect dictate that stars will shine as beacons of light? Did God create planets and decide that planets will orbit stars to house people, other life and rocks? Did early astronomical observers confuse planets in the night sky with stars? Can you ask yourself: "What is *unique* about stars which causes them to be hot and bright?"?

Why is the center, but not the crust, of Earth molten? Did God decide that objects with the most mass would make the prettiest sources of light, and therefore designate them as stars? Or, *do the properties of mass, distortion of spacetime and critical levels of pressure on atoms* determine whether a physical body in space will have its atoms converted to plasma of nuclei and electrons?

Is nuclear fusion occurring daily in the Sun? Is there an optimal size for a star in order to sustain life on an orbiting planet, so that the star burns not too fast and not too slow? Is the Sun one of those "Goldilocks" stars? Is the planet Earth within an optimum orbital path so as to be not too close and not too far away from the nuclear fusion of the Sun? If Earth weren't within that optimum orbital path, would you be reading this book? How many other, similarly sized and similarly located planets, orbiting stars similar to the Sun, are out there, capable of sustaining life?

Are we alone in the Universe? Are Adam and Eve hypothetical examples of multi-stellar human representatives? Why didn't the Bible tell us this fascinating background detail?

21. Implications

If you say there are no answers for many of these questions, why are there no such answers? If there is a question, doesn't there *have* to be an answer? Isn't God all-knowing? If God is all-knowing, then there must be answers *somewhere* to all of these questions, correct?

If there are answers to all of these questions, then, *what are the answers*? If you don't know, don't you *want* to know?

If you think rationally about the nature of religious beliefs, might that *process itself* find some answers for you—if not to the questions themselves, then to the **basis** of the questions?

If these questions cause you to be skeptical of your religious beliefs, *is it wrong for you to think for yourself*? Are you hearing voices now? Should we all stop thinking rationally because it's easier that way to believe in God and Christianity? If irrational thinking is a positive thing, then was Timothy Leary perhaps onto something in the 1960s with LSD?

Who is going to think for you, throughout your life, if it is not **you** thinking for *yourself*? What kind of example are you for children? Do you want children to always conform or can they at some point, to some degree, think for themselves? Can you? Can you share your interest in *Questioning The Word* with others? Will you?

Jack Forbes

JACK FORBES

Questioning the Word
(such as...)

Could *100,000 atheists* join your church?

Is it blasphemy to *ask questions*?

Are you a champion of blind faith against all reason?

Before life existed, what did God *do*?

Is a day a day no matter where you are?

Did Adam ever bring Eve to an orgasm?

On which of the first six days were dinosaurs created?

Why did God spare fish in his murderous flood rampage?

Where are polar bears mentioned in the Bible?

Why would God lie?

Why does God want to be *worshipped*?

Do giraffes have original sin?

Is it God's will when a person exercises free will?

If all life is predetermined, why have a steering wheel when you drive?

Would you kill for your country but not for your God?

Should we lock you up *now*, before it's too late?

Does God *always* Bless America?

When you become a soul, does that make you a *ghost*?

Is there a "One Angel, One Vote" policy, or is Heaven a dictatorship?

Have any Angels fallen *for* Grace?

If we find a Bible on Mars, did Jesus die for *their* sins too?

www.ingramcontent.com/pod-product-compliance
Lightning Source LLC
Chambersburg PA
CBHW050557300426
44112CB00013B/1954